What Ails India?

Prakash Madhusudan Apte

About the book

In "What Ails India" the Author has penned his views and suggestions for a better India. Starting with the fundamentals-the Constitution of India, the electoral system, Secularism to the reservation policy- he examines all issues involved and suggests proposals for change for a better system for our democracy, governance & administration. He also discusses the consequences of the multi religionalism the masquerades as secularism. He has suggestions about ameliorating the ill effects of rampant and unchecked urbanization that is eating away the rural economy. Lastly he talks about corruption that is most rampant in this country today and the criminalization of the political and administrative system. It is his opinion that the basic issue is the cleansing the moral fiber of the society without which no amount of law making will eradicate the evil of corruption

It is not his intention to cast aspersions on any person, class of society any religion or the political system as it exists today in India. The idea is to provide serious food for thought to the thinking people of this country.

Preface

Preface

What ails India? One cannot identify a single issue. There are many, though I have dwelt only on some like; politics, religion, urbanization, corruption, terrorism in this book.

What is more important is to identify the root cause of the malaise that has brought on these ailments. Having experienced the freedom struggle in its last phases and then the 66 years of our so called independence, I have come to the conclusion that the seed of the malaise was sown by our slavish mindset nurtured by 150 years of British rule that even our so called leaders including the first Prime Minister Jawaharlal Nehru could not get free from. Had we had more real "Visionary" leaders we could have freed ourselves from the shackles of this British slavery mindset infusing in the newly independent state fresh blood of path breaking thought and philosophy.

Let us start with the Constitution of India, a blatant 'cut and paste' version of the British constitution. Had our leaders even an iota of the 'vision' they are credited with and eulogized for, we would have looked for or looked to a country like United states of America, that had then recently attained its freedom from the British, having a multiracial and multi ethnic and mostly illiterate population, having a tradition of black slavery. I have dealt with this issue in the first chapter of this book.

Let us look at the electoral system enshrined in this "cut & Paste" constitution. It is a legacy of British not suitable for an emerging democracy of multitude of illiterate and poverty ridden population. The people divided by caste, religion and economic status can hardly be expected to vote "intelligently". They either vote ruled by their hearts or the monitory compensation promised by a candidate. I have dwelt on the electoral reforms required in this book. We must have an electoral system suited to our socio economic conditions and not adopt any template and certainly not that of the British!

Let us look at the system of administration. Blindly copying the British, like the constitution, we re-designated the I.C.S as the new I.A.S and only tinkered with the system of training the Administrators. As a result the ICS system that was designed and meant to serve as a tool to rule the 'natives' and not work for their welfare was merely adapted as a system of administration for a newly born democracy! Late Mr. J.B.D'Souza Ex. Chief Secretary of Maharashtra has dwelt extensively on this issue in his autobiography "No Trumpets No Bugles". He has noted his own anguish and unfruitful efforts to orient the I.A.S. training programmes at the Administrative staff college of India, Hyderabad towards a system to "train officers to work FOR THE PEOPLE"

Let us look at the Judiciary. Another legacy of the British. It is frequently reported that there is a backlog of legal cases extending to 20 years! Granting that the courts are short staffed, it is the inherent malaise of the system itself that leads to the 'justice delayed that is justice denied'. If one were to recollect and follow the legal cases in the United States of America, one would find that rarely does justice gets delayed beyond 2 years. Compare this to the famous case in India of a film star who allegedly in a drunken state ran over and killed nine footpath dwellers, it has taken 11 years just to frame charges and register an offence! In addition to the faulty judicial system inherited from the British the rampant corruption prevailing facilitates the rich and the famous to get away scot free! As against this, many may remember the case of the American sports star accused of the murder of his wife and his chase by the police, telecast live.

Despite all that I have said above, the largely honest and incorruptible judiciary has kept this nation alive. But for it, the politicians of all parties would have auctioned this country (as is shown in some Hindi film). Having realized that it is only the judiciary with all its recent (Supreme Court decisions) interventions to stop them from eating away the country the politicians are now bent on destroying it piece by piece, first totally corrupting the selection process of judges and now keeping all politicians above the law!!

Let us turn to the next system –our armed forces. The British establishments trained their officers to use the native soldiers as cannon fodder during armed conflicts. Their system demeaned the soldier who in fact lays down his life in any conflict leaving the higher echelons to enjoy sports like polo, have gala parties and employ the soldiers as 'orderlies' to do menial work for the officers How many of us are aware that in our armed forces the system still prevails and the soldiers are assigned to polishing the shoes and doing house work at the residences of officers! The officers who enjoy very high pay and perquisites compared to the soldiers, seldom are on the forefront of any armed conflict. Whatever victories the armed forces of the country have achieved are due to the fighting spirit and valor of our soldiers. It is a tradition in India in many martial communities to send one member to the armed forces. Yet this soldier is paid a pittance compared to the salaries of the officers, is not spared by getting fed with worm infected food, get substandard equipment like shoes, jackets, snow scooters, outdated arms defective machines like, the MIG 29, most of which have never been used in a battle but have succumbed to "accidents", having substandard coffins (all this, thanks to the corruption in the higher echelons in charge of purchase of supplies). While the common soldier suffers, the national defense academy turns out officers who engage themselves mostly in wining and dining! The most distressing fact which I brought to the notice of the government (without any result) is that the sixth Pay Commission had equated a soldier with a "peon' in a government office in determining their salaries!

I often wondered why there has never been a military coupe in India while our neighbouring countries have had many. Is it because our officers in the armed forces are not only substandard in their morale, education and 'gut' but also because they have no initiative, no brains to think and reflect upon our social and political ills and are too steeped in their 'wining and dining' good lives to take such "risks"? I sincerely hope not! Our armed forced need to be reorganized to accept the importance of the common soldier and his contribution to the defense of the country and make the officer cadre more oriented and responsive to the socio -economic conditions in the country.

Over the years, since 1974, with some formal education in 'Management', I started "Role Playing". Being a trained Architect & Town Planner, looking at any building or its interior or a new city, I put myself in the role of the designer or planner of that building or the city and imagined how I would have designed the building or planned the city, if I were to be in charge. Despite being the Planner of the New Capital of Gujarat, Gandhinagar, I did not spare even myself. I retrospected that, given the opportunity to redesign the city I would do it in an entirely different way! I have said so in my book "building of Gandhinagar : the New Capital of Gujarat"

Slowly I started imagining myself in the role of an administrator, a manager, a lawmaker, a social reformer, an educationist, a politician and even a military dictator! It helped me to formulate innovative ideas about governance, management, laws and regulations, social harmony, education of our young generation, political system, the country's foreign policy and defense. All new thoughts on these issues would only be building castles in the air unless I was deeply aware of the problems, issues, constraints and possibilities. Hence I learned to make a SWOT (strengths, weaknesses, opportunities and threats) analysis of all problems that engaged my mind.

I soon realized that if I was to offer solutions or suggestions to improve any situation, I had to make a thorough study of the problem for my suggestions to be constructive. Out of this realization I studied many laws, legislation, the constitution of India, religious tenets of Hinduism and Islam, ancient history and any issue about which I wanted to offer a suggestion that was worth a serious consideration.

Out of this mulling in the mind of current socio-political issues I started writing letters to the editors of dailies in English and Marathi language. In most cases, these were not considered "fit" for publication by the "Worthy" editors. In this respect I found the editors of Marathi dailies more receptive to my ideas and suggestions. My letters in most part were highly critical of the administration, politicians and the management of the city, state and the country. Though, Most of my letters, particularly concerning urban development issues, were not published, the constructive suggestions made therein have proved to be almost prophetic! Readers interested in knowing about those could have a look at my book titled "Urban Growth Strategies: Mumbai

Lessons" which contains my suggestions, and predictions on many urban development issues that confront a city like Mumbai.

It is my belief that my thoughts & ideas, as an Urban Development expert and an individual have been neglected and sidelined because of my constant hammering about adopting optimal and low cost solutions that would benefit the people and not the politicians, bureaucrats, technocrats and the builders. The adage that I coined, "Projects in India are undertaken for their propensity to generate kickbacks for the politicians, bureaucrats and the technocrats and any benefit accruing to the people is incidental and unintended"; though 100% true has hit them hard on the face!

I have no doubt in my mind that ultimately, in future, most of my suggestions and guidelines about urban planning & development that I have given in my book "Urban Planning & Development: an Indian Perspective" will get acceptance, despite the corrupt politicians, bureaucrats and technocrats, out of sheer need to progress. In the obituary of Mr. J.B. D'Souza, ex.Chief Secretary, Government of Maharashtra and my Guru, it is very appropriately written, "You fought the good fight, you finished the course, you kept the faith..." Like him I propose to continue to fight for sane & optimal solutions to national, state & city related issues, will finish the course and shall keep the faith.

In the proceeding pages I have penned my views and suggestions for a better India in all respects particularly to reduce corruption, bring about real secularism, ameliorating the ill effects of urbanization, improve the political situation by reforms to the constitution of India and the electoral system. It is not my intention to cast aspersions on any person, class of society any religion or the political system as it exists today in India. The idea is to provide a serious food for thought to the thinking people of this country. However in the course of this discussion if there are any thoughts, inferences, statements that hurt the sensibilities of any person I tender my unconditional apology.

I must express my gratitude to my sons Dr. Shireesh and Dr. Palash Apte for patiently reading the manuscript and offering suggestions to improve it though the issues discussed are far removed from their areas of professional specialization. My wife Suneela has always been supportive of all my writings and continued to lend her moral support .

Prakash Madhusudan Apte   September 2013..

The APTE PRINCIPLE:

"Projects in India are undertaken (by governments) for their propensity to generate kickbacks for the politicians, bureaucrats and technocrats. Any benefit accruing to the people is incidental and unintended"

Joseph Bain D'Souza
June 3 1921   September 2 2007

You fought the good fight
You finished the course
You kept the faith. . .

Politics

Is India going to the dogs?

Over the years, since the politics of power started eroding every conceivable system of governance, moral & cultural fiber of the society, this question has cropped up at private discussions.

If one were to examine objectively all the amendments made so far to the constitution of India there comes a startling realization that these ostensibly "democratic" and "public welfare" oriented amendments are purely a step towards capturing political power! Starting from extension of period of "reservations" (which now extend to all conceivable sections of the society that are claimed to be backward) to the 74th amendment delegating wide powers to the "Panchayats" and all elected bodies, all these amendments help the politician hold sway over the machinery and money of the government.

Reports submitted by government appointed commissions (Mondal-Sachhar etc) have been designed to divide the people on the basis of casts and religion with the ulterior motive of segmenting the society to create vote banks and capture political power.

A very large number of the so called "public welfare oriented" legislation at the level of the union and state governments has hardly ever been acted upon or achieved the purpose for which it was ostensibly designed (anti- dowry laws and the Urban land ceiling act are a few examples) but has achieved the real purpose for which it came into existence: to facilitate illegal gratification of all the arms of the government-bureaucracy-and the police.

Every law, every rule, every measure by the state is motivated to benefit those in power and those (industrial empires) who help sustain the political power while ostensibly pretending to do public good. While the most obscene gestures and erotic dances by so called actors on the small and big screen that corrupt millions of minds are freely permitted, a few fully clad girls are prohibited from dancing to the same "filmy" tunes at the dance bars! Petty officials "caught red handed by laying a trap" are quickly sentenced while politicians literally get away with murder! Bureaucrats, top police –income tax and other officials amass wealth far beyond their apparent sources of income while salaried middle income level employees are punished for not filing income tax returns in time!

While the common man longs for and is denied justice for years together, the top courts are kept busy with claims and counter claims of corrupt politicians seeking "Justice" and "scams" of all kinds from "Chara" to "Coal"! While gun trotting police are busy providing security to the so called "People's Representatives" and marriages of cine stars and politician's progeny, innocents are being butchered by gangs and police refuse to even file a complaint! Students demanding that merit be recognized are brutally "lathi charged" while the so called minorities demand and get away with undeserved benefits and gifts on the platter!

Every conceivable aspect of the society which can yield money or political power has been systematically and cleverly exploited by the politicians with enthusiastic help from the Bureaucrats and the top police officials. There is no system. Institution or organization in the country which has not been totally corrupted,

11

subverted and marginalized to sub serve the politician's greed for money and Power. What is so far left largely intact is the Judiciary and the institutions of excellence like the IIMs. The IITs have already been corrupted.

The time is not far when the Parliament will enact constitutional amendments to keep all its laws above the purview of the Supreme Court and in fact usurp powers to appoint judges recommended by the political party in power. Similarly there shall be no autonomy for any institution and all will have to do the bidding of whoever is the political master! One only has to read the history of the Third Reich to realize that the present political powers are following in the footsteps of Hitler of "democratically destroying Democracy"! What ails India is Politics, Religion, Terrorism & Urbanization!

25th April 2013

"What ails India is Politics, Religion, Urbanization, Corruption & Terrorism"

Sixty-Five Years of India's Independence

We have just passed 15th August 2013 a milestone in India's history. We always remember Nehru's tryst with destiny speech...."At the stroke of midnight when the world sleeps, India will awake to life and freedom, when the soul of a nation long suppressed, will find utterance".

Nehru was a dreamer, a great orator and an Idealist. But his stewardship of the nation is responsible for most of our woes. He let the Muslims stay in India as equal citizens despite the subcontinent having been divided on religious grounds. We and the world now knows the result. He dreamt of a great Industrial revolution without paying adequate attention to agriculture though even today, 70% of population lives in rural areas. The result is large scale suicides by farmers. I was greatly distressed by a recent statement from the Agriculture Minister that Farmers should now leave farming and get in to other skills! What skills?

A marginal farmer who for generations has done nothing but farming, one fine day you pay him a large amount and take over his land ostensibly for SEZ what does he do?

He spends most of his money in drinking, and lands up in Mumbai in a Zopadpatti and then by dangling the carrot of regularizing his makeshift residence, you turn him into a vote bank! This is the most sinister design of politicians! The politician has got rid of the farmer, taken over his land in the name of SEZ (Special Economic Zone) where they build ultra luxurious bungalows as in Ambi valley and get him into shanties in Mumbai so that they can undertake large capital intensive projects for housing, flyovers and Metros which generate huge kickbacks for them and turn the poor chap into their own voter!!! What diabolic scheme!

Nehru talked of peace with lofty ideals continuing with the bolt action rifle for our soldiers who were slaughtered by the Chinese in the 1961 war. We remember his speech about 'Tryst with Destiny'. Do we remember his speech on All India Radio when he was asking his army to retreat from Siachen and expressing sympathy for the people of Assam which he thought would be run over by the Chinese in a few hours? I heard the speech and it still rings in my ears. He said about Siachen that it is that part of the land "where not a blade of grass grows" So what? It is my country and my land who is he to give it away on a platter to an aggressor? And then he said (probably anticipating that the Chinese army will quickly overrun the state of Assam) "our hearts go out to our brethren in Assam"! Compare these utterances of a so called patriot and Prime Minister of a sovereign nation with what Winston Churchill said in the British Parliament when Hitler attacked England and England stood alone",.....we shall fight on the beaches, we shall fight on the landing grounds, we shall fight in the fields and in the streets, we shall fight in the hills; we shall never surrender...."

So what have we achieved in these sixty six years?

Yes, we are a stable democracy with thirteen general elections and governments of all political combinations. We are a secular

14

nation, In fact are we? We are the biggest Muslim nation. It is only a matter of time that a second partition of India will take place and even this time we will retain the "patriotic Muslims" in the divided second India . It is not the fault of Islam .A few misguided and fanatic zealots have subverted the peaceful teachings of Islam into a doctrine of terrorism. Those who do not accept Islam they say," convert them or kill them" It is the 'Sanatan Dharma' (so called Hinduism) which does not encourage fanaticism but strives for self realization" and Moksha (release) from rebirth. Shireesh, my elder son, is writing a book on rapaciousness of ancient civilizations and examines why Christianity, Buddhism and Islam spread all over the world though of far recent origin while so called Hinduism in fact shrunk and vanished from Indonesia, Thailand, sri lanka etc.

There are many causes but one of the important one is the basic teachings of sanatan Dharma which urges man to know himself, achieve self realization and union with cosmos and does not preach spread of its thought . What is Secularism? (*if interested please read my researched article on 'Secularism: a concept Abused'. on my website www.angelfire.com/indie/pmapte)* We are a multi religious nation; not a secular one; with a Sikh PM, a Muslim President (until recently), a Dalit Chief Justice and a Catholic King Maker! Our GDP growth (this foolish western concept of measuring wealth of a nation has ruined our perception of development. Even the king of Bhutan – a tiny kingdom-had a better parameter, called Gross National Happiness. also embodied in the five year plans of Bhutan) had reached 10% per year, our foreign reserves are 215 billion dollars, Indian companies have taken over more than 100 major companies abroad even in countries like the USA, UK, CHINA, Russia, Germany and so on.

There are two Indians in the List of the Richest People on Earth, (how does it help the 40% of population living below the poverty line or 100 infants dying every day of malnutrition or 80% of village women traveling average 5 km. per day just to fetch drinking water?) The richest man in Britain (what is Britain? It is not even as big as our largest state!) is an Indian. Our cities are full of shopping malls,(catering to hardly 19% of population in large cities, just go out to the garbage dumps in Mumbai at 1 am to find urchins searching for morsels of food)) fast food restaurants, multiplex cinemas, posh cars and luxury apartments. We have the fastest growing mobile industry in the world. At least 30 crore Indians have a high standard of living and high incomes. (who has cooked up these figures? It is not more than 9% of total population) They all have cars, fridges, TVs and washing machines. All this sounds so wonderful. Then why do some of us feel unhappy? You have to be a real Indian to understand that.

In 1947 India was divided into two countries. Today after 65 years we have again become two countries. Let us call them India and Bharat. The people in Bharat live in villages.(There is also a Bharat of slums in cities a Bharat which is 60% of the city population) Their livelihood depends on the rainfall because in 65 years India has not been able to irrigate enough land to give farmers a comfortable income, so every year many of the farmers commit suicide, not only in Maharashtra but even in a rich state like Punjab. If a farmer drills a bore well on his farm he cannot pump that water out because there are severe power cuts in villages.

During natural disasters like famine or floods or earthquakes, generous aid is granted by the Central government but only about 1/100 of it reaches the poor victims. This is the statement of our ex-prime minister Rajiv Gandhi) due to the corruption in the bureaucracy. Corruption exists in every part of our society.

The majority of politicians go into politics simply to make money. They justify it because they have to buy votes to get elected. Today an assembly election officially costs about 1 crore per candidate. For Lok Sabha this figure goes up to 5 crores. Even fields like education are not immune to corruption from kindergarten to universities, cash donations are required to secure a place. The scheduled castes have 50% of seats reserved for them. Only Brahmins and Kshatriyas have no benefits because they are considered upper caste.

Although we call ourselves a progressive country, we were not able to wipe out our caste system. In fact it is now so entrenched in politics that a candidate is now chosen to represent the caste or religion dominant in that area. In UP a woman who openly plays the caste card had won the election and she hopes to be a PM one day! We need a total reform on our electoral system (*if interested see my researched article on 'Indian electoral system: need for total reform' posted on my website*)

I was in Goa some time back at the invitation of "Goa Bachao Andolan " to address an invited audience of intellectuals about a new town planning act for Goa. The Andolan has succeeded in getting the government to withdraw its regional plan 2011 which had declared the entire state as an Urban area and allowed construction accordingly! Can you imagine the shamelessness of the politicians and their greed in which they sought to destroy their own mother land? The Andolan has succeeded and the Government was forced to withdraw the plan and now we quickly want to put in place a legislation which can hopefully stop such mischief in future, hopefully! But it is a small state, people are educated, love their land and are willing to sacrifice their time money and energy (the assembly that I addressed paid for the entire expenses of the event-tea, lunch and the venue from their personal donations on the spot).

It is almost impossible in Maharashtra where the politicians propose to destroy the mangroves and convert the east coast salt pan lands of 5000 hectares in Mumbai into residential areas. Remember my prediction. If these salt pans are converted and if there are torrential rains as in July 2005 whole of Mumbai will be submerged as the water will just not have any outlet to flow to the sea and god help if it is high tide time!

But all this doesn't mean I am pessimistic! In fact I pity the politicians who, despite their acumen in self survival, are unable to see the signs of boiling popular unrest, blinded by their greed for power & money and self seeking policies. The day is not far off when most of them will be seen hanging by their necks from the nearest lamp post, at least I hope so!

The Second Partition: India & Bharat

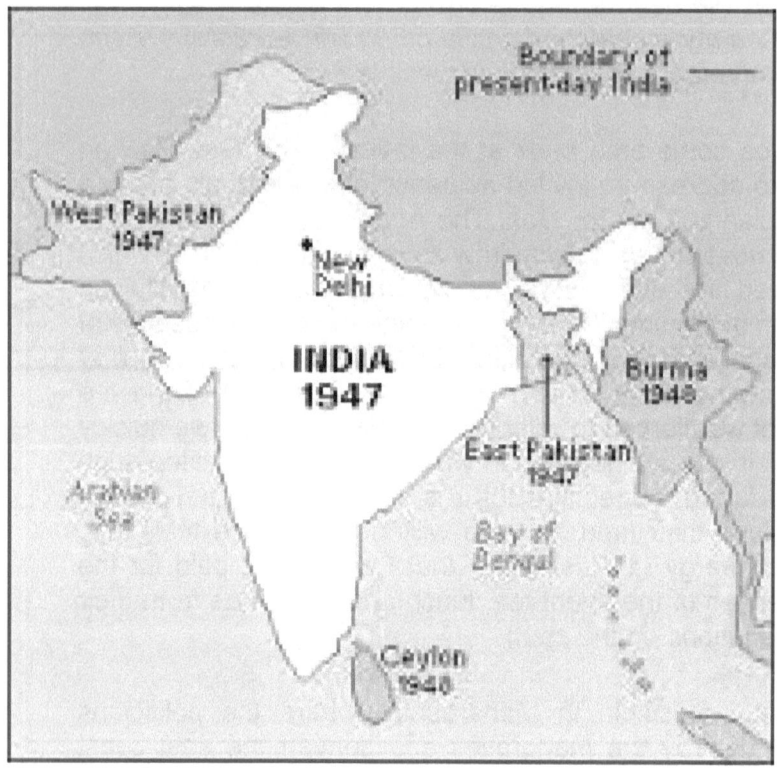

I recently read the book **The Second Partition** by Patwant Singh. The Author deals with, what in his opinion, are the basic issues of development in India. In the process, the lacunae and failings of the state (with emphasis on 'wrong doings' during the BJP-coalition rule at the centre) are brought out supported by statistics quoted irrelevantly: eg. .." as against 50 million tones of food grain produced in 1950, the figure by 2006 was over 200 million.." food production *comparison should be related to the population. If that is done the increase in production* **per capita** *will be marginally high. Similarly to compare number of universities per 1000 population in India against USA is misleading as the comparison should be of* **number of**

universities to the number of students eligible to enter a university.

The personal experience and knowledge of the Author is limited to Delhi and he depends extensively on newspaper reports and references from the media for data regarding the country as a whole. This detracts from the credence of his authority to pass comments on countrywide issues.

Despite his mostly valid criticism of the successive governments in their prioritization of developmental issues he fails to suggest even possible options to correct the imbalances or lacunae. Despite fleeting references he has not pinpointed population explosion as the central issue for all developmental efforts. He criticizes, without providing viable corrective options for most issues that he has identified. In that, this treatise has become negative with a fatalistic tone.

I think there is still hope. How?

Decelerate population growth by incentives, deterrents: irrespective of ethnicity,

Reform electoral system

Abolish reservations in education and employment

Accept village as the nodal point for developmental efforts

Discourage urbanization provide "urban" facilities in villages

Manage water as a community property, not a salable commodity

Accept supremacy of law and Judiciary over Legislature

Accept all activities as supplementary to Agriculture

But is it possible to lift up our system and politicians from the abyss that they have voluntarily fallen into? Do they have time to think about the country? Imagine our Parliament, the supreme law making body of a country, framing and passing a law within hours just for a Minister to get even with his 'Bette-Noire' (Mr. Ambados vs. Venugopal of AIIMS)!

Imagine the Coastal Regulation Zone rules for the entire country being modified to allow building within 500 meters of the high tide line **if there is a compound wall between the sea and the land plot**! All this just to accommodate an Industrialist (undeclared rulers of India) for their plot in Mumbai !

Imagine the Central Government ceiling of 5000 hectares on land for SEZ being relaxed to allow 12000 hectare land acquisition in Navi Mumbai being next door to the proposed new airport (being built at a public cost of Rs. 4800 crores, curtsey Aviation Minister), a 37 km. rail cum road bridge connecting it to Nariman Point (at a public cost of Rs. 24000 crores, curtsey Govt. of Maharashtra) and possibility of converting the 12000 hectares into 100 palatial estates of 120 hectares each with a private helipad and 9 hole golf course for the 100 richest in India (a la Ambi Valley- Lavasa)! All this aided and abated by top politicians, bureaucrats and Planners!

Last month at the Western Region Planners Conference in Navi Mumbai I delivered a Key Note address on " Impact of Liberalization: Maharashtra" The minister (Tope) had spoken before my address and had mentioned Mahatma's words (all politicians quote him but never follow his sane and down to earth advice) " India lives in its villages" I started my address by referring to his quote and said ," **Today India is dying in its villages particularly in Maharashtra where one farmer commits suicide everyday"**.

March 2008

"Manage water as a community property, not as a salable commodity"

Reforms to the Constitution of India: Rewrite

PREAMBLE

WE THE PEOPLE OF INDIA having solemnly
resolved to constitute India into a SOVEREIGN
SOCIALIST SECULAR DEMOCRATIC REPUBLIC
and to secure to all it's citizen

JUSTICE, social, economic and political
LIBERTY of thought, expression, belief, faith and worship
EQUALITY of status and of opportunity
and to promote among them all.
FRATERNITY assuring the dignity of individual and
the unity and integrity of the nation.

IN OUR CONSTITUENT ASSEMBLY the twenty-sixth
day of November, 1949, do, HEREBY ADOPT,
ENACT AND GIVE TO OURSELVES THIS CONSTITUTION

Most intellectuals and thinkers in India, feel dismay and
hopelessness at the current political, economic, and social
conditions. They, in their own fields of proficiency, are trying to
support development. But they feel increasingly frustrated in their
efforts because, the political rivalries and debasement of politics,
bureaucratic neglect, nepotism and corruption; religious, social
and linguistic strife almost nullify their efforts.

In desperation, there is a tendency to fall back on legal
remedies, by way of public interest litigation and right to
information procedure. This created an impression of excessive

21

judicial activism and the political community across the party lines was at one time almost on the point of making judiciary subservient to the executive controlled by corrupt politicians.

The lament of the Indian intellectual is well expressed in a recent book "The second Partition" by Patwant Singh. The Author deals with, what in his opinion, are the basic issues of development

But is it possible to lift up our system and politicians from the abyss that they have voluntarily fallen into? Do they have time to think about the country?

But I think there is still hope. How?

Accept supremacy of law and Judiciary over Legislature,

(unfortunately the governments are constantly indulging in subverting the supremacy of judiciary by diluting the provisions, aided by even the opposition political parties, like gaining control over appointment of judges, keeping legislators out of the perview of the supreme court by amending the constitution etc.)

reform the electoral system, decelerate population growth by incentives, deterrents: irrespective of ethnicity, accept all activities as supplementary to agriculture not the other way round, accept village as the nodal point for developmental efforts discourage urbanization; instead provide "urban" facilities in villages manage water as a community property not as a salable commodity abolish reservations (based on caste) in education and employment.

But this is easier said than done. Why? No amount of efforts to decelerate population growth, reform electoral system, discourage urbanization, assert supremacy of law and Judiciary over Legislature, and eradicate corruption can succeed under our present form of Constitution. The basic cause of the malice is in the present form of our nation's Constitution.

Despite the eulogies sung in praise of our constitution makers, the brutal & bitter truth is, it is but a "cut & paste" copy of the British constitution which was even at the time of Indian independence most ill suited for a newly born democracy with 90% population in rural areas, deprived of adequate access to education, food, shelter, employment and steeped in poverty with the nation at the bottom of the list of undeveloped countries. The only way that this country can hope to substantially contain and eradicate the ills of political, social and economic injustice is to have a new constitution, if not new, at least reform the present one substantially by amendments.

What I have laid down in my subsequent writing is an outline framework for such a reform which can be carried out by amendments to the existing constitution. The format evolves from felt need of last 65 years and should be viewed as more of an urgent & practical response to these felt needs rather than a theoretical and idealistic approach to the subject of reforms to the Constitution of India.

Constitution of India: Rewrite

Constitution of a nation is expected to embody the basic principles and reflect aspirations of its people over a long term perspective. While it may consider the socio-economic conditions at the time of the birth of the nation, the Constitution has to be futuristic. Aspirations can be limitless but Principles have to be as few as possible. In that, a Constitution should be like "Bhagavatgeeta' and not like 'Mahabharata'. Unfortunately our Constitution has become like the Mahabharata and Ramayana put together!

The king of Bhutan having decided to convert his kingdom (total population 600,000) to a democracy, appointed a constituent assembly which studied the constitutions of 85 countries before finalizing the draft for their country's constitution. But the great architects of our constitution, probably in a hurry to frame one, decided to just copy the British one without the slightest consideration for the differences in the history, traditions, size, socio-economic conditions or the level of literacy between the two countries ,instead of looking at the constitution of USA which also got its independence from the British rule.

United States of America earned its independence, also from the British rule on 4th July 1776 that is 171 years before India. The **Constitution of the United States of America** provides the framework for the organization of the country's Government. It defines the three main branches of the government: The legislative branch, an executive branch, and a judicial branch. It outlines which powers each branch may exercise, reserving for the States, numerous rights thereby establishing a FEDERAL SYSTEM for the Country. This constitution is the shortest-contains only 7 Articles (with 27 subsequent amendments)- and the oldest among any major democracy. It was adopted in 1787, and later all the States ratified it in the name of the "People"

We earned our independence 171 years after the USA. Our constitution also defines the three main branches of the government; the legislative, executive and judicial branch AND everything else under the sun, including formation of Panchayats, Municipalities (though listing formation of local self government body etc. in the State List of 7th schedule), Commissions, Tribunals, Offices & officers of government their emoluments etc.etc. All this extends to 395 articles and over 90 amendments! It establishes a UNITORY FORM of government making the President a titular head (cut & paste from British constitution-replace word Queen by President) complete with house of Lords (read Rajya Sabha/Vidhan Parishad) and House of Commons (read lokasabha/Vidhansabha). It is surprising (and thankfully fortunate) that the so called great Architects of this constitution did not provide for all the Ex-Maharajas of all the erstwhile states in India to be the Presidents of the country in rotation!

Why is the constitution so "epic"? Simply because it is NOT a constitution but a format of an 'Act' something that our great "architects", being lawyers by education, were best suited to formulate! Except for absence of a first section containing 'definitions', it is a classic format of an ACT trying to cover everything under the sun on the subject. Unfortunately, those

24

great architects of the constitution could not even frame a 'good' act as it is self contradictory! Despite placing the formulation of local self government authorities like Panchayats, Municipalities etc in the "state list" it goes on to define their formulation, scope, duties etc.! To gloss over this basic fault and at the behest of an enthusiastic but inexperienced Prime minister it also has the 74 th amendment to "establish" Panchayat Raj!

Suggested Reforms:

I suggest 9 basic reforms. These are explained in brief below. A more detailed explanation will appear in the following when those of the Articles of the Indian Constitution that in my opinion require reform are listed and explained with the numbers referring to the Article number in the present constitution and the *relevant part of the Article reproduced in italics.*

A) Change the name of the country from Bharat to Hindusthan. this is the name by which the country was known historically
B) Make the country a Federation of States.

This will afford greater autonomy to the states so essential in a large multi- religious and multi- lingual country

C) Reform the mode of election and powers of the President

President being the ultimate authority and commander in chief of the armed forces, he/she should be a person of eminence, non political and need not be always guided by the decisions of the council of ministers of the majority coalition in power

D) Abolish the upper houses of Parliament & State Assemblies and reform the mode of election and composition of the LokSabha and VidhanSabhas

The blind copy of the British system of having a Rajya Sabha & Vidhan Parishads (House of Lords) is neither relevant to Indian socio economic conditions nor serves any useful purpose apart from being a huge burden on the state exchequer. At least 50% members of the Lok Sabha & Vidhan Sabhas should be elected from amongst non political eminent professionals.

E) Establish a permanent economic commission charged with the responsibility to ensure and constantly correct the economic system so that there is no concentration of wealth and means of production to the common detriment. Despite platitudes to the contrary in article 39 there is no system put in place to ensure its intents which is suggested to be corrected by establishment of a permanent economic commission.

F) Freedom not to adopt a common civil code

If the country is to be really 'Secular' -meaning not subscribing to ANY religious doctrine and NOT subscribing to ALL religions as is happening today with state holidays for ALL religious festivals- people should have the option to follow tenets of their religion in their social behaviour and all consequences arising there from.

G) Independence and supremacy of the Judiciary which shall not be at any times made subservient to the Legislature or Executive.

Neither the President nor the parliament without a 4/5 [th] majority of the sitting members shall have the right to make any changes in the system or the rights and scope of the judiciary as formed by the constitution.

H) The posts of Governors of the state can be abolished In view of the suggested Federal form of government. In case of any constitutional crisis or failure of a state government, the Chief Secretary of the State shall be the chief Executive of the state acting under the instructions of the President. He shall arrange to have a popular government elected through the election commission as may be prescribed in the constitution .

J) All provisions in the present constitution relating to subjects within the state list shall be removed. There is also no need to

26

include in the constitution the provisions for appointment of Attorney general, Public Service Commission

Article wise suggestions:

The preamble to the Constitution reads:

1.   *(1) India, that is Bharat, shall be a Union of States.*

This should read, " India that is Hindustan shall be a Federation of States"

'Bharat', 'Aryavarta' etc. are the ancient names found in "Purina" associated with Aryan race. Since the days of Mughal, and the British rule, the country was known as 'Hindustan' and as the partition of the subcontinent named one part 'Pakistan' the remainder should continue to have the historic name 'Hindustan'. India is in fact an anglicized version of Hindustan

Many of the problems now being faced in the relationship between the state and central governments can be avoided by making the country a "Federation of States' that would give a very large measure of autonomy to the states and meet a long standing aspiration of the states.

The original draft of the constitution, as it came into effect in 1950, had the words SOVEREIGN DEMOCRATIC REPUBLIC in the first line. The words SOCIALIST and SECULAR were inserted by the controversial 42nd amendment. Through the same amendment, the words unity of the nation were changed to unity and integrity of the nation. The amendment was pushed through by Indira Gandhi in 1976, when she had dictatorial powers.

The words 'Socialist' and 'Secular' introduced by Indira Gandhi should be removed and the original words 'Sovereign Democratic Republic' should be retained.

Right to Freedom of Religion

25. *(1) Subject to public order, morality and health and to the other provisions of this Part, all persons are equally entitled to freedom of conscience and the right freely to profess, practice and propagate religion.*

In view of the above provision in the constitution, there is no need to have the word 'Secular'. But in this provision the last but one word *'propagate'* should be removed in order to eliminate religious conversion through compulsion or enticements.

30. *(1) All minorities, whether based on religion or language, shall have the right to establish and administer educational institutions of their choice.*

Why should the Constitution itself create differences within the populace by introducing terms like *'religious', 'language'* minorities as it professedly does not differentiate between the populace on the basis of religion, cast or creed and promises equal opportunities and treatment to all? Hence In the above article 30 the word *'all minorities'* should be replaced by *' any group of people'* . As a consequence, the Minority Commissions at central and state level can be abolished and use of word 'Minority' in such context be prohibited.

32. *Without prejudice to the powers conferred on the Supreme Court by clauses (1) and (2), Parliament may by law empower any other court to exercise within the local limits of its jurisdiction all or any of the powers exercisable by the Supreme Court under clause (2).*

In view of the country being a Federation of States, the Parliament can legislate to allow the High Courts of all the States to exercise the powers of the Supreme Court and in effect give a Supreme Court to each state commensurate with its greater autonomy.

39. *The State shall, in particular, direct its policy towards securing—(c) that the operation of the economic system does not result in the concentration of wealth and means of production to the common detriment;*

This article is but a mere platitude. The economic system has not only resulted but continues to foster concentration of wealth and means of production to the common detriment. Article 39 must incorporate appointment of an 'Economic Systems Reform Commission' at the Federal level which will not only formulate policies for the effective achievement of the intents of this article but will be a permanent watchdog for the purpose.

44. *The State shall Endeavour to secure for the citizens a uniform civil code throughout the territory of India.*

In a multi religious and ethnic country like India it may not be possible to have a common civil code. Article 44 should therefore be expanded to add,

' *citizens are free to follow a code prescribed by their religion provided that any disputes, civil or criminal offenses arising out of such following shall be judiciable under the tenets of the concerned religion and its enforcement shall be overseen by the Federal or State law enforcement agencies. If no remedies are available under the religious tenets for such civil or criminal disputes or offenses, then the common civil code shall apply'.*

50. *The State shall take steps to separate the judiciary from the executive in the public services of the State.*

This article 50 should be rephrased to read, ' The state shall take steps to separate the judiciary from the executive

' *and Legislature in all matters of the state and the powers of the Judiciary as prescribed in the constitution shall be inviolable and not subject to change except by the consent of 4/5 th majority of the members of the Parliament'.*

51A. It shall be the duty of every citizen of India—(a) to abide by the Constitution and respect its ideals and institutions, the National Flag and the National Anthem;

Insert words *'salute'* before the words *'National Flag '* and *'sing'* before the words *'the National Anthem'*

This article should be expanded to read *'and those who fail to do so shall forfeit the citizenship, fundamental rights guaranteed under the constitution and protection under the law of the land. The current National Anthem-Jana Gana Mana..- was written in honour of the king of England. Originally "Vande Mataram" was to be the National Anthem, but because of staunch opposition of the Muslims to sing any song in praise of anyone/anything but "Allah" Pandit J. Nehru managed to make "Jana Gana.Mana" as the National Anthem. Hence it should be abandoned and "Vande Mataram."be made the National Anthem.*

52. There shall be a President of India.

53. (1) The executive power of the Union shall be vested in the President and shall be exercised by him either directly or through officers subordinate to him in accordance with this Constitution.

(2) Without prejudice to the generality of the foregoing provision, the supreme command of the

defense Forces of the Union shall be vested in the President and the exercise thereof shall be regulated by law.

54. The President shall be elected by the members of an electoral college consisting of—

(a) the elected members of both Houses of Parliament; and

(b) the elected members of the Legislative Assemblies of the States.

All the Judges of the Supreme Court, Chief Justices of the State High Courts and the Chief Secretaries of all state governments and Speakers of the Parliament and state assemblies shall form a committee (to be later on converted into an Advisory council) to scrutinize the names of candidates for the office of the

President of India. The eligibility of a person to be a candidates shall be as prescribed in the present constitution except that such a person shall not have been a member of any political party during the preceding 15 years. The committee shall shortlist the names of the candidates after an open discussion and shall submit it to the Election Commission. The commission shall then conduct an election by secret ballot .The electorate shall comprise of all the members of the Parliament and the state assemblies. A person elected as a president shall not be eligible to be a candidate at any future elections for the office of the President of India

74. *2[(1) There shall be a Council of Ministers with the Prime Minister at the head to aid and advise the President who shall, in the exercise of his functions, act in accordance with such advice:] 3[Provided that the President may require the Council of Ministers to reconsider such advice, either generally or otherwise, and the President shall act in accordance with the advice tendered after such reconsideration.]*

The President, shall thereupon call a meeting of this Advisory Council and after presenting his arguments against the bill referred to him for assent by the council of ministers shall put the issue to vote and shall act in accordance with the majority opinion of the Advisory council.

79. There shall be a Parliament for the Union which shall consist of the President and two Houses to be known respectively as the Council of States and the House of the People.

80. *(1) 1[2*** The Council of States] shall consist of—*

(a) twelve members to be nominated by the President in accordance with the provisions of clause

(3); and (b) not more than two hundred and thirty-eight representatives of the States 3[and of the Union territories.]

31

(3) The members to be nominated by the President under sub-clause (a) of clause (1) shall consist of persons having special knowledge or practical experience in respect of such matters as the following, namely:-

Literature, science, art and social service.

There shall be only one house of the people. 50% of the members shall be elected by general election while the remaining 50% shall be representatives of the state nominated by the state governments consisting of persons of accomplishments (not being members of any political party 15 years prior to their nomination) in the fields of but not limited to, Agriculture, Economics, Medicine/health care, Rural/Urban development, Trade & Commerce, Manufacturing & Industry, Transport & communication, Information Technology, Engineering & Architecture, Management, Earth Sciences, Education, Water management etc. Members to be nominated by the President as under present article 80(3) 1 shall remain unchanged. The composition of the only house of the state assemblies shall be similarly composed of 50% members elected by the people and 50% nominated by the state government as in case of the house of people of the Parliament.

122. *(1) The validity of any proceedings in Parliament shall not be called in question on the ground of any alleged irregularity of procedure.*

The validity of any proceedings in Parliament can be called in question by an appeal to the Supreme Court.

132. *(1) An appeal shall lie to the Supreme Court from any judgment, decree or final order of a High Court in the territory of India, whether in a civil, criminal or other proceeding, 1[if the High Court certifies under article 134A] that the case involves a substantial question of law as to the interpretation of this Constitution.*

However such an appeal in all other matters can lie with the Supreme Court only if referred to it by the High Court of the state but not at the request of either parties to any dispute

153. There shall be a Governor for each State:

There shall not be a of Governor for any state.

168. *(1) For every State there shall be a Legislature which shall consist of the Governor, and—*

(a) in the States of 2[Andhra Pradesh,] Bihar, 3*** 4[Madhya Pradesh], 5*** 6[Maharashtra],

7[Karnataka], 8***9[and Uttar Pradesh], two Houses; (b) in other States, one House.

The legislature of a state shall be constituted by the same process as the Parliament and shall consist of only one house as suggested for Article 80 above.

169. *(1) Notwithstanding anything in article 168, Parliament may by law provide for the abolition of the Legislative Council of a State having such a Council or for the creation of such a Council in a State having no such Council, if the Legislative Assembly of the State passes a resolution to that effect by a majority of the total membership of the Assembly and by a majority of not less than two-thirds of the members of the Assembly present and voting.*

(5) The members to be nominated by the Governor under sub-clause (e) of clause (3) shall consist of persons having special knowledge or practical experience in respect of such matters as the following, namely:—Literature, science, art, co-operative movement and social service.

This provision can be eliminated.

330. *Reservation of seats for Scheduled Castes and Scheduled Tribes in the House of the People.*

335. *The claims of the members of the Scheduled Castes and the Scheduled Tribes shall be taken into consideration, consistently with the maintenance of efficiency of administration, in the making of appointments to services and posts in connection with the affairs of the Union or of a State: 1[Provided that nothing in this article shall prevent in making of any provision in favour of the members of the Scheduled Castes and the Scheduled Tribes for relaxation in qualifying marks in any examination or lowering the standards of evaluation, for reservation in matters of promotion to any class or classes of services or posts in connection with the affairs of the Union or of a State.]*

There shall be no reservation of seats.

No relaxation under any circumstances can be made in qualifying marks in any examination or lowering of standards of evaluation in favour of any person on the grounds of his cast, creed, religion, economic or social backwardness etc.

361. *(1) The President, or the Governor or Rajpramukh of a State, shall not be answerable to any court for the exercise and performance of the powers and duties of his office or for any act done or purporting to be done by him in the exercise and performance of those powers and duties:*

Every individual irrespective of his rank or status shall be answerable in a court of law.

368. *2[(1) Notwithstanding anything in this Constitution, Parliament may in exercise of its constituent power amend by way of addition, variation or repeal any provision of this Constitution in accordance with the procedure laid down in this article.]*

1[**370.** (1) *Notwithstanding anything in this Constitution,— (a) the provisions of article 238 shall not apply in relation to the State of Jammu and Kashmir*

The constitution can be amended by the Parliament by a 4/5 [th] of its members voting in favour of such amendment and 4/5 [th] of the members of the President's Advisory Council endorsing such an amendment.

Article 370 should be deleted.

I have prepared this document to generate a healthy discussion on a subject of vital importance to the progress of a nation. There is no intention to cast any doubts on the intentions and integrity of or disrespect to the Architects of our present constitution of India. I tender my unqualified apology if the foregoing has created any such impression of insult or disrespect.

1st November 2008

Appendix

Some of the relevant articles from the Constitution of India as in force now are reproduced here for ready reference

Constitution of India:

The original draft of the constitution, as it came into effect in 1950, had the words *SOVEREIGN DEMOCRATIC REPUBLIC* in the first line. The words *SOCIALIST* and *SECULAR* were inserted by the controversial 42nd amendment. Through the same amendment, the words *unity of the nation* were changed to *unity and integrity of the nation*. The amendment was pushed through by Indira Gandhi in 1976, when she had dictatorial powers.

Constitution is a living document, an instrument which makes the government system work. Its flexibility lies in its amendments.

1. (1) India, that is Bharat, shall be a Union of States.

24. No child below the age of fourteen years shall be employed to work in any factory or mine or engaged in any other hazardous employment.

Right to Freedom of Religion

25. (1) Subject to public order, morality and health and to the other provisions of this Part, all persons are equally entitled to freedom of conscience and the right freely to profess, practice and propagate religion.

30. (1) All minorities, whether based on religion or language, shall have the right to establish and administer educational institutions of their choice.

32. (3) Without prejudice to the powers conferred on the Supreme Court by clauses (1) and (2), Parliament may by law empower any other court to exercise within the local limits of its jurisdiction all or any of the powers exercisable by the Supreme Court under clause (2).

39. The State shall, in particular, direct its policy

towards securing—(c) that the operation of the economic system does not result in the concentration of wealth and means of production to the common detriment;

44. The State shall endeavor to secure for the citizens a uniform civil code throughout the territory of India.

50. The State shall take steps to separate the judiciary from the executive in the public services of the State.

51A. It shall be the duty of every citizen of India—(a) to abide by the Constitution and respect its ideals and institutions, the National Flag and the National Anthem;

52. There shall be a President of India.

53. (1) The executive power of the Union shall be vested in the President and shall be exercised by him either directly or through officers subordinate to him in accordance with this Constitution.

(2) Without prejudice to the generality of the foregoing provision, the supreme command of the defense Forces of the Union shall be vested in the President and the exercise thereof shall be regulated by law.

54. The President shall be elected by the members of an electoral college consisting of—

(*a*) the elected members of both Houses of Parliament; and

(*b*) the elected members of the Legislative Assemblies of the States.

74. 2 [(1) There shall be a Council of Ministers with the Prime Minister at the head to aid and advise the President who shall, in the exercise of his functions, act in accordance with such advice:] 3 [Provided that the President may require the Council of Ministers to reconsider such advice, either generally or otherwise, and the President shall act in accordance with the advice tendered after such reconsideration.]

76. (1) The President shall appoint a person who is qualified to be appointed a Judge of the Supreme Court to be Attorney-General for India.

79. There shall be a Parliament for the Union which shall consist of the President and two Houses to be known respectively as the Council of States and the House of the People.

80. (1) 1 [2 *** The Council of States] shall consist of—

37

(*a*) twelve members to be nominated by the President in accordance with the provisions of clause

(3); and (*b*) not more than two hundred and thirty-eight representatives of the States 3 [and of the Union territories.]

(3) The members to be nominated by the President under sub-clause (*a*) of clause (1) shall consist of persons having special knowledge or practical experience in respect of such matters as the following, namely:-

Literature, science, art and social service.

109. (1) A Money Bill shall not be introduced in the Council of States.

110. (1) For the purposes of this Chapter, a Bill shall be deemed to be a Money Bill if it contains only provisions dealing with all or any of the following matters, namely:—

(*a*) the imposition, abolition, remission, alteration or regulation of any tax;

(*b*) the regulation of the borrowing of money or the giving of any guarantee by the Government of India, or the amendment of the law with respect to any financial obligations undertaken or to be undertaken by the Government of India;

(*c*) the custody of the Consolidated Fund or the Contingency Fund of India, the payment of moneys into or the withdrawal of moneys from any such Fund;

(*d*) the appropriation of moneys out of the Consolidated Fund of India;

(*e*) the declaring of any expenditure to be expenditure charged on the Consolidated Fund of

India or the increasing of the amount of any such expenditure;

(*f*) the receipt of money on account of the Consolidated Fund of India or the public account of

India or the custody or issue of such money or the audit of the accounts of the Union or of a State; or

(*g*) any matter incidental to any of the matters specified in sub-clauses (*a*) to (*f*).

122. (1) The validity of any proceedings in Parliament shall not be called in question on the ground of any alleged irregularity of procedure.

132. (1) An appeal shall lie to the Supreme Court from any judgment, decree or final order of a High Court in the territory of India, whether in a civil, criminal or other proceeding, 1 [if the High Court certifies under article 134A] that the case involves a substantial question of law as to the interpretation of this Constitution

134. (1) An appeal shall lie to the Supreme Court from any judgment, final order or sentence in a criminal proceeding of a High Court in the territory of India if the High Court—(*c*) 1 [certifies under article 134A] that the case is a fit one for appeal to the Supreme Court:

143. (1) If at any time it appears to the President that a question of law or fact has arisen, or is likely to arise, which is of such a nature and of such public importance that it is expedient to obtain the opinion of the Supreme Court upon it, he may refer the question to that Court for

consideration and the Court may, after such hearing as it thinks fit, report to the President its opinion thereon.

153. There shall be a Governor for each State:

168. (1) For every State there shall be a Legislature which shall consist of the Governor, and—

(*a*) in the States of 2 [Andhra Pradesh,] Bihar, 3 *** 4 [Madhya Pradesh], 5 *** 6 [Maharashtra],

7 [Karnataka], 8 *** 9 [and Uttar Pradesh], two Houses; (*b*) in other States, one House.

169. (1) Notwithstanding anything in article 168, Parliament may by law provide for the abolition of the Legislative Council of a State having such a Council or for the creation of such a Council in a State having no such Council, if the Legislative Assembly of the State passes a resolution to that effect by a majority of the total membership of the Assembly and by a majority of not less than two-thirds of the members of the Assembly present and voting.

(5) The members to be nominated by the Governor under sub-clause (*e*) of clause (3) shall consist of persons having special knowledge or practical experience in respect of such matters as the following, namely:—Literature, science, art, co-operative movement and social service.

212. (1) The validity of any proceedings in the Legislature of a State shall not be called in question on the ground of any alleged irregularity of procedure.

239. (1) Save as otherwise provided by Parliament by law, every Union territory shall be administered by the President acting, to such extent as he thinks fit, through an administrator to be appointed by him with such designation as he may specify.

1 [PART IX

THE PANCHAYATS

1 [**PART IXA**

THE MUNICIPALITIES

243. Subject to the provisions of this Constitution, the Legislature of a State may, by law, endow— (a) the Municipalities with such powers and authority as may be necessary to enable them to function as institutions of self-government

244. (1) The provisions of the Fifth Schedule shall apply to the administration and control of the Scheduled Areas and Scheduled Tribes in any State 1 *** other than 2 [the States of Assam 3 [, 4 [Meghalaya, Tripura and Mizoram]]].

(all lands to be state owned & leased to individuals to reap the land value benefit)

247. Notwithstanding anything in this Chapter, Parliament may by law provide for the establishment of any additional courts for the better administration of laws made by Parliament or of any existing laws with respect to a matter enumerated in the Union List.

SERVICES UNDER THE UNION AND THE STATES

C HAPTER I.—S ERVICES

308. In this Part, unless the context otherwise requires, the expression "State" 1 [does not include the State of Jammu and Kashmir].

PART XV

ELECTIONS

324. (1) The superintendence, direction and control of the preparation of the electoral rolls for, and the conduct of, all elections to Parliament and to the Legislature of every State and of elections to the offices of President and Vice-President held under this Constitution 1 *** shall be vested in a Commission (referred to in this Constitution as the Election Commission).

330. Reservation of seats for Scheduled Castes and Scheduled Tribes in the House of the People.

335. The claims of the members of the Scheduled Castes and the Scheduled Tribes shall be taken into consideration, consistently with the maintenance of efficiency of administration, in the making of appointments to services and posts in connection with the affairs of the Union or of a State: 1 [Provided that nothing in this article shall prevent in making of any provision in favour of the members of the Scheduled Castes and the Scheduled Tribes for relaxation in qualifying marks in any examination or lowering the standards of evaluation, for reservation in matters of promotion to any class or classes of services or posts in connection with the affairs of the Union or of a State.]

352. (1) If the President is satisfied that a grave emergency exists whereby the security of India or of any part of the territory thereof is threatened, whether by war or external aggression or 1 [armed rebellion], he may, by Proclamation, make a declaration to that effect 2 [in respect of the whole of India or of such part of the territory thereof as may be specified in the Proclamation].

361. (1) The President, or the Governor or Rajpramukh of a State, shall not be answerable to any court for the exercise and performance of the powers and duties of his office or for any act done or purporting to be done by him in the exercise and performance of those powers and duties:

368. 2 [(1) Notwithstanding anything in this Constitution, Parliament may in exercise of its constituent power amend by way of addition, variation or repeal any provision of this Constitution in accordance with the procedure laid down in this article.]

1 [**370.** (1) Notwithstanding anything in this Constitution,— (*a*) the provisions of article 238 shall not apply in relation to the State of Jammu and Kashmir

2 [**371.** 3 * * * *(2) Notwithstanding anything in this Constitution, the President may by order made with respect to 5 [the State of Maharashtra or Gujarat], provide for any special

responsibility of the Governor for—(*a*) the establishment of separate development boards

List II—State List

5. Local government, that is to say, the constitution and powers of municipal corporations, improvement trusts, districts boards, mining settlement authorities and other local authorities for the purpose of local self government or village administration.

1 TWELFTH SCHEDULE

(Article 243W)

1. Urban planning including town planning.

2. Regulation of land-use and construction of buildings.

3. Planning for economic and social development.

4. Roads and bridges.

5. Water supply for domestic, industrial and commercial purposes.

6. Public health, sanitation conservancy and solid waste management.

7. Fire services.

8. Urban forestry, protection of the environment and promotion of ecological aspects.

9. Safeguarding the interests of weaker sections of society, including the handicapped and mentally retarded.

10. Slum improvement and up gradation.

11. Urban poverty alleviation.

12. Provision of urban amenities and facilities such as parks, gardens, playgrounds.

13. Promotion of cultural, educational and aesthetic aspects.

14. Burials and burial grounds; cremations, cremation grounds; and electric crematoriums.

15. Cattle pounds; prevention of cruelty to animals.

16. Vital statistics including registration of births and deaths.

17. Public amenities including street lighting, parking lots, bus stops and public conveniences.

18. Regulation of slaughter houses and tanneries.

"...a Constitution should be like "Bhagavatgeeta' and not like 'Mahabharata'. Unfortunately our Constitution has become like the Mahabharata and Ramayana put together!"

Indian Electoral System: Need for a Total Reform

India is a constitutional democracy with a parliamentary system of government. At the heart of the system is a commitment to hold regular, free and fair elections. These elections determine the composition of the government, the membership of the two houses of parliament, the state and union territory legislative assemblies, and the Presidency and vice-Presidency

Under the present electoral system, the country has been divided into 543 Parliamentary Constituencies, each of which returns one Member of Parliament (MP) to the Lok Sabha, the lower house of the Parliament. The size and shape of the parliamentary constituencies are determined by an independent Delimitation Commission. However, under a constitutional amendment of 1976, delimitation was suspended until after the census of 2001. This has led to wide discrepancies in the size of constituencies, with the largest having over 25,00,000 electors, and the smallest less than 50,000.

45

The Constitution puts a limit on the size of the Lok Sabha of 550 elected members. There are provisions to ensure representation of scheduled castes and scheduled tribes, with reserved constituencies where only candidates from these communities can stand for election. There is a proposal to reserve one third of the seats for female candidates. The president can nominate 2 members to the Lok Sabha and 12 members to the Rajya Sabha (Upper House of Parliament). Elections to the Vidhan Sabhas (State Legislative Assemblies) are carried out in the same manner as for the Lok Sabha election. The President is elected by the elected members of the Vidhan Sabhas, Lok Sabha, and Rajya Sabha, and serves for a period of 5 years.

Elections in India are events involving political mobilization and organizational complexity on an amazing scale. In the 2004 election to Lok Sabha, there were a total of 5398 candidates from recognized national and state parties, other registered parties and independent candidates. Out of total 675 million registered voters, 380.4 million people voted. The Election Commission employed over 40,00,000 people to manage the election. A vast number of civilian, police and security forces were deployed to ensure that the elections were carried out peacefully. The direct cost of organizing the election amounted to over Rs. 13 billion.

The present electoral system in India, (as also its constitution) is the legacy of the former British rulers. The system, called 'First Past the Post system' (FPTP) is also called the Westminster model, as it originated in the political culture of United Kingdom. Due to the vast former British Empire, it is till now the most common electoral system in the world with almost two billion people casting their votes for assemblies in 68 countries including United States of America, Canada, many Caribbean countries; island states in the Pacific and almost all the former British colonies in Asia and about 18 countries in Africa.

The basic principle of FPTP is that the **winner is the candidate** with the plurality – **relative majority** - of all valid votes. The Constituent Assembly of India in 1948, debated for almost three years the issue of which electoral system should be adopted, before finally choosing the FPTP electoral system. It was chosen mainly to avoid fragmented legislatures and to help the formation of stable governments - stability being a major consideration in a developing country with widespread poverty and illiteracy. Ironically, the system has failed to provide a stable government as is evident from the events in recent times.

The pitfalls of the Indian electoral system become evident at every general election. The ever-increasing **role of money and muscle power** has made mockery of the elections shamming the concept of democracy. The system (first-past-the-post system) ensures that a **person with a vote bank of around 25-30 per cent can be sure of victory**. The **character and public service record of the candidates** have become irrelevant. Elections are fought almost entirely on **communal and caste considerations**. The **seat-vote distortion**, is a major drawbacks of the system. **True representation of people** is not possible in the present electoral system.

To give an example, in 1991 in Tamilnadu, the AIADMK-Congress alliance got only 40 % votes but swept the state by winning 99% (232 of the 234) seats and the opposition DMK despite having secured 34% votes won just 9% (2)seats! In 1996, the AIADMK front won only 1.5% seats and the DMK 98.5% though the difference in the votes they got was just 6%! In 2001, the AIADMK front got 31% votes but 72% seats and the DMK front got 30.4 %votes but only 12% seats! The difference in votes was just 0.6%, but the difference in seats was 60%! Similarly, the overall results of elections to the Lok Sabha have never been proportional. Because the candidate who obtains the most votes, but not necessarily a majority of votes polled, is declared elected, votes can often be divided by 'setting up' candidates of the same caste, religion, or region against each other.

The electoral system in India requires a drastic reform to ensure that a **truly proportional representation of the people** is assured and **distortions between the percentage of votes polled and seats won is minimized.** It is therefore necessary to replace the first-past-the-post system that we have today by a system that can truly reflect the will of the people by having a proportional parity between votes polled and seats won by any

47

political party. The existing system of elections by simple majority gives **greater importance to the individual candidate than the political party**. Elections are not an exercise in choice among various political party programmes. The so-called merits of the candidates assume a decisive role. **Elections become personality-oriented instead of being issue-oriented.**

In our present electoral system political parties, instead of **'selling'** their programmes and policies try to **"buy"** the constituency **by using religion, caste or linguistic arithmetic** and search for candidates who fit in that arithmetic. Consequently, the parties tend to be a collection of individuals, who can walk in or walk out of the party at their sweet will. Political parties perhaps start with subordination to the social structure in the hope that they will be able to manipulate the system later so that primacy of the political parties will emerge. This has proved to be an illusion so far.

The existing electoral system has only helped in the maintenance of the superiority of the social structure over the functioning of the political parties thus diluting party programme. The candidate who wins on the basis of his local "qualifications" is expected by the voters and supporters to 'benefit' them for the support! In the process the party becomes secondary.

This kind of individualism, corrupts the body politic, and loosens loyalties in the party. The greatest flaw of the present electoral system is that there is little relationship between the electoral performance of a party and its strength in the Parliament or the Assembly. For example, the Congress party in several general elections to the Parliament obtained far more seats than the percentage of votes secured by it. This defect can be remedied only by a total reform of the present electoral system. The alternative is a Proportional Representation (PR) system.

PROPORTIONAL REPRESENTATION SYSTEM

The basic principles underlying proportional representation elections are that all political groups in society deserve to be represented in our legislatures **in proportion to their strength**

in the electorate and **all voters deserve representation**. In other words, everyone should have the right to fair representation. In a proportional representation system, legislators are elected in multimember districts instead of single-member districts, and the number of seats that a party wins in an election is in direct proportion to the amount of its support among voters. The PR system was devised to solve the many problems caused by plurality-majority voting systems. **As a rule, PR voting systems provide more accurate representation of parties,** which can help in better representation for political and racial minorities, women, and greater likelihood of majority rule.

The PR system allocates the seats according to the proportion of votes received by the various parties or groups of running candidates. Thus, if the party wins 40% of the vote in a 100 member assembly, they receive 40 of the 100 seats -- or 40% of the seats. If another party wins 20% of the vote, it gets 20 seats, and so on.

Proportional representation voting (PR) is the real alternative to plurality-majority voting. Among advanced western democracies it has become the predominant voting system. In Western Europe, 21 of 28 countries use proportional representation including Austria, Belgium, Cyprus, Denmark, Finland, Germany, Greece, Ireland, Luxembourg, Malta, the Netherlands, Norway, Portugal, Spain, Sweden, and Switzerland.

Proportional representation (PR) with all its variations, is an attempt to secure a representative assembly reflecting, with more or less mathematical exactness, the various divisions in the electorate. The immediate gain for India, if PR is adopted, will be the end of vote garnering by playing the race, religion, caste and language cards. The phenomenon of `independent candidates, with wavering loyalties, will come to an end. The strength of the Indian political system will depend on the strength of party system; and it is essential to opt for an electoral system which helps in the strengthening of the party system. **Proportional representation system is better than the prevailing simple-majority system.**

A variety of different formulas exist for accomplishing the actual allocation of seats to the parties. One of the simplest seat allocation formulas is called the "largest remainder formula." In this approach, the first step is to calculate a 'norm', which is determined by dividing the total number of valid votes in the district by the number of seats. For example, if 100,000 votes were cast and ten seats are to be filled, 100,000/10 = 10,000 is the norm. The norm is then applied to the votes that each party receives and the party wins one seat for each whole number produced. So, if the Congress party received 38,000 votes, it is divided by 10,000 to produce three seats – with a remainder of 8,000. After this first allocation of seats is complete then the remainder numbers for the parties are compared and the parties with the largest remainders are allocated the remaining seats. For example, if 2 seats remain to be allocated and the Congress and BJP, have the largest remainders they get the seats. Ultimately all the parties end up with the number of seats that, as closely as possible, approximates their percentage of the vote.

Types of PR Systems: Party List Voting
Party list voting system is by far the most common form of proportional representation. Over 80% of the PR systems used worldwide have some form of party list voting. It is used in most European democracies and in many new democracies, including South Africa.

In this system, Legislators are elected in large, multi-member districts. Each party puts up a list of candidates equal to the number of seats in the district. Independent candidates may also run, and they are listed separately on the ballot as if they were their own party. On the ballot, voters indicate their preference for a particular party and the parties then receive seats in proportion to their share of the vote. So in a five-member district, if the Congress wins 40% of the vote, they would win 2 of the 5 seats. The two winning Congress party candidates would be chosen according to their position on the list.

Open List

Most European democracies now use the open list form of party list voting. This approach allows voters to express a preference for particular candidates, not just parties. It is designed to give voters some say over the order of the list and thus which candidates should get elected. Voters are presented with random lists of candidates chosen by a party. Voters do not vote for a party directly, but cast a vote for an individual candidate. This vote counts for the specific candidate as well as for the party. So the order of the final list completely depends on the number of votes won by each candidate on the list. The most popular candidates rise to the top of the list and have a better chance of being elected. This system is used in Finland and widely considered to be the most acceptable version of open list voting.

Mixed Member Proportional Representation

Mixed-member proportional representation is more popularly known as "the German system." It is an attempt to combine a single-member district system with a proportional voting system. Half of the members of the legislature are elected in single-member district plurality contests. The other half are elected by a party list vote and added on to the district members so that each party has its appropriate share of seats in the legislature. Proponents claim that mixed-member proportional voting (MMP) is the best of both worlds: providing the close constituency ties of single-member plurality voting along with the fairness and diversity of representation that comes with PR voting.

Germany implemented MMP more than 50 years ago. In the 1990s New Zealand abandoned its traditional single-member plurality system for MMP. Hungary also adopted this approach. Most recently, the newly formed parliaments of Scotland and Wales used this system for their first elections. Mexico combines its MMP with a presidential type of government.

There is absolutely no doubt that the present FPTP system in India does not reflect the true will of the people. Therefore, claims of any political party that it has received the "mandate" from the electorate are not only erroneous but amount to a blatant lie because its **majority in terms of seats** is not necessarily reflected in its **securing a majority of votes.** The BJP in 2004 won 25.41% seats against its vote share of 22.16%, in 1999, 33.5% against a vote share of 23.75%. The Congress (INC) in 2004 won 26.7% seats against a vote share of 25.63% while in 1999 it won 20.9% seats against a vote share of 28.3%. Such distortions can be eliminated in a Proportional Representation system.

But the most important factor in favour of a total reform in the present FPTP system is that the voter, in the present system, votes for **A CANDIDATE** on the basis of his **religion, caste, language or capacity to offer monetary rewards** to his supporters. The electoral process becomes a contest between candidates on the basis of their personal influence, monetary and 'muscle' might and religious-language-caste affiliations! **This has to change in a multi racial-religious-linguistic - caste society in India to promote national integration.**

A simple Proportional Representation System (without any list) will ensure that,

Political parties will get seats in proportion to the votes they receive reflecting truly the will of the electorate,

Voting will have to be for the programmes of the parties and not for a candidate,

Race, religion, caste of individual candidates will not play any part in the election process,

As the candidates will be nominated by the party their performance will determine their continuance as members of the assembly or Parliament,

Political parties, by law, can be made to nominate members in proportion to the religious, linguistic, caste and sex composition of the state or country avoiding need for reservations of any kind,

52

A healthy political party system may develop,

Unhealthy and unethical political alliances cannot take place before the elections. Political parties will be compelled to fight elections on the basis of their programmes and enter into coalition only after elections for the purpose of forming a government.

All intellectuals in India need to seriously reflect on this issue and work actively for a complete reform of our present electoral system.

"There is absolutely no doubt that the present FPTP system in India does not reflect the true will of the people. Therefore, claims of any political party that it has received the "mandate" from the electorate are not only erroneous but amount to a blatant lie."

RESERVATIONS POLICY: A CONCEPT ABUSED

Before the Muslim invasion of India (starting in Sindh in 715 AD by Mohammad Bin Qasim in 980 AD by Mohamad of Gazni and around 1191 AD when Mahmud Ghori captured Delhi), Islam as a religion did not exist in this country. Divided in various kingdoms ruled by kings from different dynasties, India was a multitude of religions. Buddhism existing as a small sect before 270 BC where after its propagation was greatly aided by king Ashoka during his rule between 270 to 312 BC. Jainism existed even before 599 BC.

The most ancient was the Vedic religion believed to have existed since around 4000 BC. Vedic religion honored a number of deities that were tied in function and domain to nature, divine powers that controlled various aspects of the natural world. There was Vayu, the wind god, Agni, the fire god, Indra, the god of thunder and king of the gods, and others. Through the fire sacrifice, Agni accepted prayers and oblations from the worshipers to the realm of the gods, to whom the sacrificer appealed for worldly assistance.

In early Vedic times, members from the same family could follow different occupations according to any profession he liked best,. Each member was at liberty, though born of the same parents, to follow different disciplines of knowledge. Over the years, when the Vedic Aryans, having grown in numbers, spread throughout the whole country, they divided themselves into four classes according to their different qualities (gunas) and actions(karmas) in order to structure their society upon a sound basis. This fourfold classification came to be known as 'Chaturvarna'. The 'Brahmin' engaged in pursuit of knowledge and study of scriptures, the 'Kshatriya' was the warrior class protecting his people against foreign aggression, the 'Vaishya' engaged in trade and commerce and the 'Shudra' engaged in providing menial services to the society. It was a division based on occupation voluntarily chosen by a person and one could change it had he the abilities.

I quote here from our scriptures to show how a man's class could be promoted or degraded according to his good or bad qualities and action and was not necessarily a permanent division by birth.

"Man gets into a higher class by virtuous deeds."(Mahabharata, Shanti Parva)

"A Shudra attains the rank of a Brahmin and Brahmin sinks to the level of a Shudra. The same can be true in the case of the children of a Kshatriya or a Vashya." (Manu Samhita)

"By doing religious deeds men of a lower class rise to the higher class and should be considered as such. By doing irreligious acts, men of a higher class fall to the lower one and should be treated so." (Apastambha Samhita)

Even a Brahmin, guilty of wicked acts and taking bad food, falls from Brahminhood and becomes a Shudra. Even a Shudra, whose soul has been purified by virtuous deeds and who has his senses controlled, is to be served as a Brahmin." (Mahabharata)

"Not by high parentage, nor by class but by deeds alone one becomes a Brahmin. Even a chandala, O Yudhisthira, becomes a Brahmin by good conduct." (Mahabharata)

Unfortunately, this occupational classification, over the ages, became a mandatory hereditary compulsion and 'Shudras' who served the society came to be regarded as untouchables and prohibited from academic pursuits and became a downtrodden community. Many social reformers till 19th century AD worked for the betterment of the socio-economic status of these 'untouchables' and achieved a fair measure of success. Their efforts involved imparting education and enlightening this section of the society and simultaneously 'brainwashing' the members of the higher class to abandon those age old ideas of 'superior' and 'inferior' class. The apostle of such social reformers was Mahatma Gandhi.

The political leaders however felt that the efforts of the social reformists in removing this evil of untouchability and backwardness of a majority of the people of Indian society were too slow and will not achieve results unless the evil was uprooted by 'law' and special privileges were granted to these lower sections of the society. This reasoning prompted the framers of the Indian constitution to enshrine the provisions of 'Reservations' to the particular class by including them in 'Schedules' appended to the constitution for a period of 25 years which was later, by an amendment, extended by another 25 years and now appears to have become a permanent feature of the constitution. The 'Schedules' continue to name 'Casts' and Tribes' that are to be given this privileges, though the constitution itself declares as its objective, creation of a 'Castless' society!

The provision under the constitution for scheduled castes/scheduled tribes/other backward classes are:

SC/STs

Art. 338:- National Commission of SC/STs

Art. 335, Art. 15(4) & Art. 16(4-A):- Different Provisions for reservation in services.

Art. 46:- 'Same as above'

Apart from these, the political reservation for SC/STs is provided in Art. 330 & 332, Notification for SC (Art. 341) & ST (Art. 342). Additional provisions for the Tribes are given in the V & VI schedules of the Indian constitution. Abolition of untouchability is provided in Art. 17.

OBCs

Art. 340 - National Commission for OBCs (As of yet two commissions had been formed one in 1953 and one in 1977, they are Kaka Kalelkar and Mandal commission respectively)

Art. 15(4) & Art. 16(4) and Art 16(4-A):- Different provision for reservation in services

Though the makers of Indian Constitution were against communal reservations, they made an exception in the case of the SC/ST and OBC for historical reasons and included Part XVI- "Special provisions relating to certain classes." Even then, provisions in this part were intended for a temporary period. With regard to backward classes, Article 340 empowered the President to appoint a commission to investigate their social and educational conditions and to make appropriate recommendations for their emancipation. Hence, the Mandal commission, whose recommendations led to reservation of 27 per cent of Government jobs for them, in addition to the existing one for the SC/ST. Article 340 was "not" intended for the Muslims or the Christians.

The main two privileges accorded are,

1. priority in admissions to educational institutions/Universities without fulfilling the minimum requirements prescribed for admission to even specialized disciplines like Engineering & Medicine and
2. preference in employment and promotion in government/ semi government jobs over all the others without fulfilling the minimum qualifications pr for recruitment to these jobs.

These privileges have created a clamor amongst sections of the society to get themselves classified as Scheduled Casts (SC), Scheduled Tribes (ST), Other Backward Classes (OBC) by obtaining false certificates (giving rise to corruption amongst those authorized to issue such certificates) and also demand by other sections for such privileges on grounds of a 'minority' status (by Muslims) and economically backward communities. On the other hand, these have created resentment amongst the higher classes whose members, despite being far better performers in education and qualification; fail to get admissions in the educational institutes or land jobs with the government.

One might argue that such a reservation policy –called 'Affirmative Action'-is practiced even in the most developed country like United States of America. There is however a major difference in the two. In the USA, those to whom the Affirmative action applies (mostly Afro-Americans) constitute only 12.1% of the total population (1999 U.S.Bureau of Census). Hence there is little or no resentment created among the non Afro-American population as the granting of privileges to the Afro-Americans does not even marginally reduce the opportunities of the rest of the Americans.(this provision of affirmative action has recently been abolished) While in India the classes to whom the reservation policy applies constitutes almost 74.5% of the total population!

The Reservation policy in India has resulted in;

A dangerous lowering of standards of academic education to benefit the new 'privileges' class (SC/ST/OBC candidates, though just meeting the minimum grade required to 'pass' an examination – in that too having received concession for being an SC/ST/OBC- score over the most brilliant of the students in getting admission to specialized careers like Engineering or Medicine)

Consequent lowering of standards in recruitment to jobs in government services, (resulting in an abysmal lowering in the quality of services provided by governmental institutions)

A feeling of arrogance and complacency among the class leading to considering the privileges as their 'birth right'(because of the belief that whether or not one has any merit he is bound to get a preferential treatment due to his status as an SC/ST/OBC.)

'Hereditary' claims for these privileges due to extension in the time limits set originally for the operation of Articles 338 & 340 of the constitution. (Though after having received preferential treatment in education and jobs and having advanced socially and economically, the next generation continues to claim the same preferential treatment!)

Ironically therefore, the Reservation policy has created a new 'privileged' class far above the highest that existed in the Vedic religion replacing one caste system with another!

My contention is that, it may be good in principle to 'right' the 'wrong' (reservation policy for the down trodden) but it is disastrous in practice as it in fact replaces one wrong with another! One can't cure discrimination with discrimination. It is not the principle that is under question but the way it is put into practice. In our democratic state we must in fact shun and abhor the words 'Reservation' and 'Privileges'. If all the subjects of this state are equal in the eyes of law and justice how can we even think about reservations and privileges?

What is the way to ensure that those who were downtrodden for ages are given a place of honour as due to every individual in our society? The answer is my concept of 'Affirmative action".

Affirmative action means, positive steps taken to increase the representation of the hereto downtrodden classes in areas of employment, education, and business from which they were historically excluded. The purpose of Affirmative action is *not* to compensate for past wrongs, offset unfair advantage or reward the undeserving. Its purpose is to change institutions so they could comply with the nondiscrimination mandate of the Indian constitution.   Affirmative action will not involve *preferential* selection (as in the present Reservation policy) on the basis of Caste, Religion, tribe or Backwardness of any kind. Affirmative action decisions will generally not be based on quotas, nor will they give any preference to unqualified candidates. And they are not supposed to harm anyone through "reverse discrimination."

To achieve this objective I suggest following measures,

1.   Free and best possible education to all the children of the underprivileged classes. To achieve this, in urban areas, I suggest that all private schools double their tuition fees and run the school in second or third shift with the best possible teaching staff exclusively for the underprivileged.

2.   In rural areas running of special schools for these children and payment of adequate daily allowance to the family to compensate for the loss of income due to the loss of a 'working hand'

3.   Having given these special facilities ,judge all students on par and allow the selection of the best as per their merit for higher education (preference being given to the under privileged ,merit being equal)

4.   Recruitment to all jobs purely on merit and qualification without lowering performance standards (preference being given to the underprivileged, merit being equal)

5.   The special facilities for education should be continued for as long as it may take for the educational levels among the 21+ age group of the underprivileged to achieve parity with the rest.

Apart from these caste/religion based reservation there is another kind of reservation that has come into being: Elected Representatives Reservation. Members of all elected bodies consider themselves as a "Special Class" to be given preferential treatment in every service from rail/air tickets to exemption from paying road tolls, traffic regulations . In fact they have come to regard themselves as "masters" who are not bound by laws and regulations that govern the common man. This kind of "Reservation" is the most dangerous and needs to be abolished immediately.

Over the years the Reservation Policy has been used more to achieve political ends rather than for up liftment of the under privileged. It is used by the politicians to create and maintain 'Vote Banks'. Without a total reform in the Electoral system of the country this policy will remain only as a tool in the hands of politicians to attain their own ends.

Reservation policy is like treating the symptoms of a social evil, not its remedy. Remedy is to elevate the educational,

intellectual and economic level of the underprivileged by education and instill confidence in them to compete with others as equals.

"Affirmative action means, positive steps taken to increase the representation of the hereto downtrodden classes in areas of employment, education, and business from which they were historically excluded. The purpose of Affirmative action is not to compensate for past wrongs, offset unfair advantage or reward the undeserving. Its purpose is to change institutions so they could comply with the nondiscrimination mandate of the Indian constitution."

Reorienting Indian Policy Perspectives:

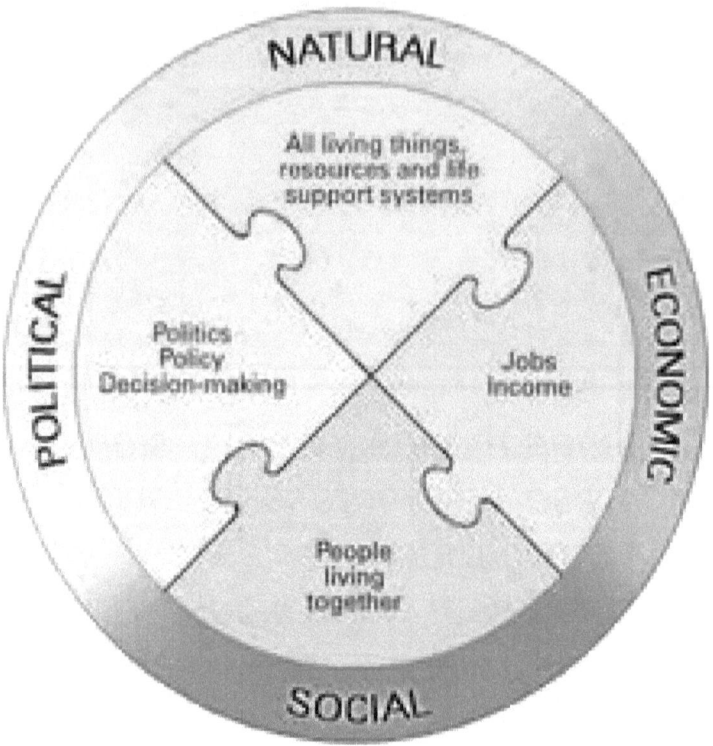

It is high time the Government of India reorients its policies on Education, Health, Environment and Foreign relations

Education - A major failure of the state is its inability to educate all its citizens. We need a revolutionary new policy on primary education in rural areas. Primary education needs to be reoriented towards vocational guidance like improved methods of agriculture, vegetable and cash crop farming, all aspects of agricultural produce ranging from farming to marketing, farming based industries etc. We can do away with teaching of History, restrict teaching of mathematics, science and geography to the extent that it relates to rural occupations and emphasize rural hygiene and health care education.

Health - The Rural poor remain very vulnerable to water-borne diseases. Malnutrition in some parts of India is worse than that in sub-Saharan Africa. Rural population must be reeducated about the importance of traditional medicine and weaned away from its attraction to the allopathic medicine ('injectibles' propagated by self seeking medical practitioners) and encourage recourse to Herbal, Ayurvedic and Homeopathic medicine by rural population and take drastic measures to completely stop indiscriminate use of herbs like Aloe-vera, Tulsi, Neem etc and fruits like Strawberry, Amla in cosmetic preparations for use by the urban elite! Teaching of medicine in traditional systems must be encouraged by establishing institutions in rural areas.

Environment - There are no two opinions that our major rivers are polluted; our groundwater aquifers rapidly depleted. Efforts by 'green' experts (Singh, Mishra, Hazare) working in rural areas to conserve water, encourage rain water harvesting, social forestation, must be actively supported and replicated. This may mean curtailing our enthusiasm for large river dams and canal projects which mainly benefit the rich farmers (who are actually the absentee politicians) and the large construction companies and in turn the bureaucrats and government officials and politicians who are the beneficiaries of the kick backs from the construction companies.

Foreign affairs - India faces threats from the rise of radical Islam and from a politically ambitious military in Pakistan and Bangladesh, by the unwillingness of the Maoists to whole-heartedly enter the democratic process in Nepal, and a fresh cycle of terrorism based on the discontent of the Tamils in Sri Lanka. Our long-term national interest will be served only if we take a brutally self-serving attitude to all foreign policy matters and ally with any global power, if it suites our national interests. No one has appointed our nation as the keeper of world peace or conscience nor human rights protection. USA's war on Iraq was self serving (to ensure supplies of oil) Russia's war with some of the erstwhile USSR states is self serving and Pakistan's harping on Kashmir is the result of hatred of India The motto of our foreign policy should be like that of North Korea which looks to self interest !

Sharp, clear, forward-looking thinking in these spheres of governance is vital for the future of India. This thinking is not likely to emerge from the current political class. A special responsibility devolves on the Indian information media. "One desperately hopes that, in the months and years to come, some of the space currently reserved for the game of cricket and for the lifestyles of billionaires and film stars will be used on finding ways and measures of making the citizens of India more healthy, better educated, environmentally aware, and safe

"It is high time the Government of India reorients its policies on Education, Health, Environment and Foreign relations"

Religion

(Pseudo) Secularism:

The British regime in India, after a rule for over 150 years, ended on August 1947. The subcontinent was divided into two nations, India and Pakistan. The demand of Muslims for a separate nation resulted in creation of West Pakistan and East Pakistan comprising of areas having a majority of Muslim population. Nizam- a Muslim ruler of the then Hyderabad state (comprising parts of the current state of Andhra Pradesh) though ruling over a majority of non-Muslim population, tried to annex his state to Pakistan. Popular uprising and timely help from India, mainly by the then Minister of Home affairs- Vallabhbhai Patel- avoided creation of another island of a Muslim State within the Indian territory. Jammu and Kashmir (J&K), a state (with a majority of non-Muslim population in Jammu and Muslims in Kashmir) ruled by a non-Muslim king –Harisingh- chose to be a part of India . This was resented by the rulers of the newly created state of Pakistan and it first sent mercenaries and later its own regular army to occupy J&K. The armed conflict ended with a unilateral cease fire ordered by Jawaharlal Nehru. The state of J&K to date remains divided between India and Pakistan.

The Indian freedom movement leaders like Mahatma Gandhi, Jawaharlal Nehru, Abul Kalam Azad and Vallabhbhai Patel were not in favour of division of the sub continent on the basis of religion and preferred to have India as a single nation with multi-religion population. Yet, when Barrister Jinah, the supreme leader of Muslims, insisted upon and got a Muslim Pakistan created, they tried to crystallize the concept of a multi-religion population nation for the rest of India, by calling it a "Secular" state. Sardar Vallabhbhai Patel was the lone voice which argued that since the subcontinent was divided on the basis of religion and Pakistan was created as the 'Holy land' for Muslims, logically, all Muslims from the subcontinent should shift there. But leaders like Mahatma Gandhi and Nehru who were highly idealistic wanted to create a nation of multi- religion population. They dominated the Constituent Assembly entrusted with the task of framing a constitution for India and succeeded in their objective of creating a 'Secular' state. The thinking of the framers of the Indian Constitution, mostly educated in the British education system in England, could not go beyond the British Parliamentary system, and resulted in declaration of India as a Sovereign Secular Republic, on 26th January 1948 by a Constitution that used the British constitution as a 'Template'.

It is my contention that, had the framers of the Indian constitution been able to remove the 'British blinkers' and take a look at the then emerging nations, they would have realized that the constitution of the United states of America (a nation liberated from the British empire) was THE right 'Template' to use for framing the constitution of a newly liberated state like India. Had they the 'vision' they are credited with and constantly eulogized for by our political leaders, they would have unshackled themselves from the age old serfdom of their erstwhile masters-the British- and adopted as a template the constitution of the United States of America, a nation that liberated itself from the British bondage. The course of history of the Indian democracy since 1947, could have broken a new path had the constitution been modeled on that of the United States of America.

What did the framers of Indian Constitution had in mind when the state was declared as 'Secular'? What is the meaning of Secularism? Secularism is defined in the Webster dictionary as: "A system of doctrines and practices that rejects any form of religious faith and worship" or "The belief that religion and ecclesiastical affairs should not enter into the function of the state especially into public education." The concept was readily accepted by the non-Muslim population of India being steeped in tradition of tolerance and devoid of religious dogmatism. Acceptance of the concept was helped greatly by the fact that a majority of the non-Muslim population was loosely knit together by a loose fabric of customs, mores, traditions and placid acceptance of realities of life and not by a specific and dogmatic religious book of 'commandments'. That is why the non-Muslim population accepted without any protest a law enacted in the 1950s that prohibited them from having more than one wife, though, the history of ancient India from the 'Ramayana' & 'Mahabharata' till the nineteenth century is replete with examples of kings ,courtesans and commoners having more than 1 wife. Lord Krishna himself is said to have had 16000 wives, (the legend is a gross distortion of facts, but that is a subject for another 'Reflection'!). The non-Muslim population accepted such laws though they infringed on their age old tradition and religious scriptures because they realized the social desirability of such laws in the changed socio-economic times.

But can India be really Secular with over 150m. of its population, **(larger than the total population of Pakistan)** being Muslim? What does Islam say about secularism?

"There is no doubt that secularism contradicts Islam in every aspect. They are two different paths that never meet.... whoever chooses Islam has to reject secularism. Secularism is... clear unbelief (Kufr)... based on separating religion from all the affairs of this life ... it rules by law and regulations other than Allah's laws... secularism rejects Allah's rules with no exception...." (Al Jumuah [The Friday Report], vol III, no. 10.)

"Secularism can never enjoy a general acceptance in an Islamic society.,... slogans like "no religion in politics and no politics in religion" ... deceive people with democratic slogans like

"personal freedom" and "people governing people." ..means that people come first and no place is made for the ruling of Allah. This is why secularism is clear Kufr, .. secular systems should be rejected by Muslims." (Dr. Yusuf al-Qaradawi from 'Al-Hulul al Mustawradah wa Kayfa Jaat `alaa Ummatina')

Fortunately such fanatical thoughts have been rejected by most Islamic societies and democracies have been instituted in countries like Iran, Egypt, Iraq, Afghanistan, etc.

How is the concept of Secularism enshrined in the Indian constitution actually put into practice?

It is commonplace to see wall hangings of (Hindu) gods and goddesses in government offices with floral offerings. State functions are inaugurated by performing 'Puja"-(god worship)-

National holidays are observed for special occasions of all religions including one for the birthday of Prophet Mohammed (though it is not observed as a holiday in any Muslim country), and chanting of excerpts from Hindu religious books. State leaders, in their official capacity annotate gods in temples, to pray for rains or better harvest. Religious festivals are held within the precincts of government offices, An entire state government stops working for 10 days at a stretch to celebrate a religious festival. The state officially refers to people other than Muslims as a national 'majority' and Muslims as a national 'minority',

Is this Secularism?

Over the years, due to compulsions of politics, appeasing the religious, caste and linguistic group votes has made the state a de-facto 'all religion state' instead of a 'secular' state. Any minority group, linguistic, religious or otherwise which is a sizable 'vote bank' is wooed and appeased by the political parties and the government as a means to gain political power to ultimately control the state. With regional political parties gaining ground and pitch forking themselves in the position of becoming 'king makers' for forming a government at the federal level, secularism as a tenet of the state is fast disappearing and making way for a 'please all' attitude. In the process minority religious groups with dogmatic and fanatic leanings extract maximum advantages from the state and the tolerant keep tolerating.

If India is to be a really Secular state in the true sense of the word, then I think that,

There can be a religious, linguistic or economic minority but no national minority or majority. No population group can be considered as a 'majority' or 'minority' and accorded privileges on those grounds. Hence, no special privileges can be accorded to any so called minority group.

The state shall not interfere with the religious beliefs and customs of any group and cannot make laws to restrict, prohibit or promote them.

Conversely, no religious group can subvert, ignore, protest or defy any regulations formed for the welfare of the state or dishonour the state flag, emblem or anthem on the grounds that these go against its religious tenets. If they do so they shall forfeit their citizenship and nationality and the privileges that go with it.

No religious group can indulge in activities or teachings prejudicial to the sovereignty and safety of the state on the grounds that its religious tenets require it of them. The state shall not discriminate between one religious group and other in dispensing justice and privileges.

Conversely, no religious group can jeopardize the interests of the state on the plea that its religion does not permit a certain behaviour and observance, though required in the interest of the state and prescribed by law.

The state cannot declare a national holiday for any religious festival. There can be only two holidays, Independence day and Republic day. Holidays for all other festivals can be made as optional holidays that may be observed by the people of any faith, total number of holidays being restricted to 10 in a year

There cannot be any special or privileged treatment by the state or any 'reservation' for any group on the basis of it being a religious minority or majority. The state must be an equal opportunity employer.

"Over the years, due to compulsions of politics, appeasing the religious, caste and linguistic group votes has made the state a de-facto 'all religion state' instead of a 'secular' state. "

Depiction of Hindu gods in nude

सरस्वती

Vedic scriptures that are the fountain head of Sanatan Dharma refer to only three gods, Brahma the Creator, Vushnu the Preserver and Mahesha the Destroyer. All other icons like Rama, Krishna, Bhairava and others are "Avatars" or human forms of these gods but NOT GODS.

In recent times many painters and artist have faced heat for painting nude Shiva and other Hindu deities. Many of them have claimed and have been supported in such claims by so called

Scholars that Shiva, for example, is depicted in nude every day in the form of Shivalinga or in his "Avatar" as Bhairava.

As a student of Indian Architecture & allied arts for the last 54 years, I have never ever come across nude depiction of the gods (Brahma-the creator, Vishnu-the preserver, and Mahesha-the destroyer) in Indian or Hindu mythology. The Scholars of Indian iconography need to dispel, once for all the myth and mischief, particularly of the visual artists (Hussain, Das, J.Choudhary, Atul Dodiya et al) that Hindu gods have been represented in nude in our ancient sculptures. The nude depictions that these Painters perhaps allude to, are in fact those of Gandharva, Kinnara or Apsara (celestial actors of performing arts) or Yaksha –a human creation of Brahma. To say that, because the "Shiva Linga" (male sexual organ) has been historically openly displayed, it amounts to Shiva's depiction in nude, is to display one's abysmal ignorance and arrogance. Artists must have liberty of expression but liberty should not become a license to 'libel'.

In this context Let me dispel the myth of "Shivalinga". The expression does not mean 'linga (sexual organ) OF Shiva'. The word Shiva in Sanskrit means 'sacred' or 'pure' (Pavitra). The 'Linga' partially penetrated into 'Yoni' (female sexual organ) is a depiction of the force ('Shakti') that sustains this world by procreation. It has no connection whatsoever with Shiva who is the god of destruction and not of creation. This Icon was venerated by the followers of 'Shakta Panth' and not by the worshippers of Shiva. While the vandalism indulged into by common people at the obscene depiction of their deities however deplorable, is at least understandable, the wanton obscene depiction by the Artists raises doubts about their real intentions.

Many so called scholars have referred to "Purana" to substantiate their claims that Shiva has been depicted in nude in Indian iconography. Perhaps these scholars are not aware that Puranas fall into the category of Hindu scripture known as *Smrti* (recollected tradition) and vary from place to place and from time to time. They are usually written in Sanskrit and normally tell of the genealogies of gods, kings, and saints, and contain assorted narratives, stories, and legends. Legends cannot be quoted as authentic evidence.

The three main Hindu deities, Brahma, Vishnu, and Mahesh are never ever depicted naked, displaying their genitalia, in any Indian or Hindu iconography. The photographs referred to by such scholars in support of their contention are those of "Bhairava" or "Bhikshantana", a human incarnation of lord Shiva and not of god Shiva. The form of Bhairava is considered to be fierce, one that infuses more fear than love towards Lord Shiva. Bhairava is known to be a naked mendicant or follows the same iconographic appearance as Bhikshatana where he is depicted ash smeared and naked. Lord Shiva descended to the earth in the form of Bhairava.

If in the eyes of such scholars vandalism of some Hindus against such depiction is reprehensible, no less reprehensible are the attempts of the so called scholars to misrepresent and misguide the people through a gullible or publicity crazy print media into making them believe that the Hindu gods were traditionally depicted in nude!

In his reference to "Shiva the destroyer of ignorance" Mr. Vithal C. Nadkarni (Times of India) refers to "Purana", un aware of the fact that Puranas fall into the category of Hindu scripture known as *Smrti* (tradition) and vary from place to place and from time to time? They are usually written in Sanskrit and normally tell of the genealogies of gods, kings, and saints, and contain assorted narratives, stories, and legends. Legends cannot be quoted as authentic evidence.

The three main Hindu deities, Brahma, Vishnu, and Mahesh are never ever depicted as naked displaying their genitalia in any Indian or Hindu iconography. The photograph published with the article is that of "Bhairava" and not "Bhikshantana", a human incarnation of lord Shiva and not of god Shiva himself. The form of Bhairava is considered to be fierce, one that infuses more fear than love towards Lord Shiva. Lord Shiva descended to the earth 18 times in the form of Bhairava. The photograph published accompanying the article by Vithal C Nadkarni is that of "Urdhvajanu" dancing Bhairava with 8 arms depicted in the Andal temple at Belur (12th Century AD Hoysala dynasty). It is probably reproduced from the book 'Nataraja in Art, Thought &

Literature' by C.Shivarama Murthy (National Museum New Delhi) page 270

Bhikshantana is known to be a naked mendicant or follows the same iconographic appearance as Bhikshatana where he is depicted ash smeared and naked with 4 arms. He is so depicted in a temple at Thanjavur (11th century AD Chola dynasty). This icon in a photograph is available in the book referred to earlier on page 112. If in the eyes of the author, vandalism of Janajagruti followers is reprehensible, no less reprehensible are the attempts of the so called scholars to misrepresent and misguide the people through a gullible or publicity crazy print media into making them believe that the Hindu gods were traditionally depicted in nude!

Freedom of Artistic Expression?

Husain's work over the years has conclusively proved that he is a "compulsive" creator of images that have offended Hindus. Paritosh sen displays his abysmal ignorance of Hinduism and Hindu art when he talks of nudity and eroticism in our temples. No Hindu god or goddess has ever been depicted in nude in ancient painting, sculpture or any art except by Husain!. All such images are of "Yaksha" and /or "Kinnar" couples. Husain has, with persistent and cynical regularity depicted in objectionable forms, Hindu goddesses, Bhartmata, and anything that should be revered by Hindus and Indians. If he has the strength of his conviction and supporters like Akbar Padamsee and Gieve Patel why is he afraid of facing the law suites? Artistic "freedom" does not mean "liberty" to offend others.(this article was written before the death of M F Hussain).

"The three main Hindu deities, Brahma, Vishnu, and Mahesh are never depicted naked, in any Indian iconography"

Urbanization

Urban Planning in India: Need for a New Strategy

Urban planning as currently practiced in India is mostly concerned with planning the use and development of land in cities for the benefit of the Politicians, Bureaucrats and the Developers. Development is merely a euphemism for land exploitation. The 74th Constitutional Amendment is a mere "paper tiger" that promises decision making authority to the elected representatives of the people, but in reality is fragrantly violated by promulgation of notifications by the state government to permit land development to suite the politician.

Perception of Urbanization

"India lives in villages" an oft-repeated adage needs to be modified to read 'India dies in its villages' as evidenced by suicides by farmers in Maharashtra. The First Five Year Plan declared, "..equality and social justice will have little content unless the production potential of the community is substantially raised." All the subsequent plans visualized the role of cities in raising the 'production potential'(economic goods) totally ignoring production of food

75

grains. Our Minister in charge of Agriculture had shamelessly advised the agriculturists to "leave" agriculture and take up other occupations! According to him, food, after all, can be purchased and imported from other countries. Creation of Special Economic Zones was important even at the cost of agricultural lands.

The Seventh Five Year Plan observed, "Urbanization is a phenomenon which is part and parcel of economic development in general. Certain activities are best performed in agglomeration of people. Planning of urban development should essentially be supportive of the economic development in the country, state or sub-region, be it in agriculture.... It is important to time investments in urban services and shelter to coincide with investments in agriculture... Industrial location policy must be made to sub serve regional and urban planning." In practice urban development was encouraged at the cost of rural development and agriculture

The Task Force on Planning of Urban Development appointed by the Planning Commission asserted in 1983 "It would be idle to imagine that rapid rise in rural population through demographic growth can be absorbed in agriculture and still ensure growth of productivity and total production." Such one sided view that did not include agro-based industry and production systems as "Agriculture" was responsible for destroying the importance of agriculture and plan allocations for it and belittled the contribution of Agriculture to the development of a country. The Eighth Five Year Plan identified small and medium towns as the thrust areas as important links between the village and the large cities. The mid-term appraisal of the 11th Five Year Plan emphasizes healthy growth of smaller towns TO EASE THE PRESSURE ON METROS and NOT to be the service centres for the rural areas!

Land Policy

Urban planning in India is largely concerned with exploitation of land. The Indian Constitution recognizes, acquisition, holding

76

and disposal of property' as a fundamental right. This ideology was negated by the enactment of Urban Land (Ceiling and Regulation) Act 1976.

Delhi Master Plan, Chandigarh, Gandhinagar and Navi Mumbai were all based on public ownership of land for the urbanizable land. In Chandigarh & Gandhinagr however an attempt was made to retain the rural character around the new towns by the enactment of the 'Periphery control Act'. Unfortunately in case of Chandigarh the bifurcation of the state of Punjab by creation of Haryana necessitated establishment of new capitals for both states putting an end to the periphery control act. In case of Gandhinagar, either the imbecility or greed of the Consultants to the Gandhinagar Urban Development Authority resulted in declaring the entire area between Ahmedabad & Gandhinagar as "Urban" destroying not only the character of the new capital city but also the rural hinterland. Public ownership of the land within the city limits of Gandhinagar thus failed to achieve the land policy objectives.

Current Perspective of Urbanization and Urban Planning

The Eleventh Five Year plan states that "cities will be the engines of economic growth and the realization of an ambitious goal of growth in GDP depends fundamentally on making Indian cities much more livable, inclusive, bankable, and competitive." What about the villages? Can those not be the engines of economic growth?
It should be noted in this context that the World Development Report - 2009 clearly states that ...even people who start their lives far away from economic opportunity (cities) can benefit from the growing concentration of wealth in a few places. The way to get both the benefits of uneven growth and inclusive development is through economic integration.

Is there really any profound and sophisticated scholarship bringing Asia to the forefront of the mainstream dialogue? If there is, is it not percolating because it is restricted to the Academics unaware of the dynamics of the practicing fraternity?

Urban Planning: Need to Plan with the Poor.

Most often, in India, people who live in the slums have other people planning for their lives. As a result, what they get is not planned with them but what other people plan for them. Most slum redevelopment projects in India have brought the issue of community participation in development decision-making into sharp focus. Redevelopment of Dharavi in Mumbai for example, revealed a complete lack of regard for the life styles of an affected community's input into key decisions that would have far reaching implications for their lives. It is an example of how tragically wrong things can go when communities are not consulted by those charged with execution of such projects.

Be it Dharavi in Mumbai or development in Navi- Mumbai it often leads violent protests making headlines in the media. We have become accustomed to regular media reports of such "service delivery" protests. At the heart of the issue appears to be the problem that people are not being listened to by the concerned authorities and the state.

A recent research conducted in South Africa by the 'Community Agency for Social Enquiry' with funding support from the Ford Foundation probed whether community participation is working; especially in the way municipalities interact with marginalized residents in terms of their housing strategies. The research hoped to improve communication between local government authorities and marginalized residents.The research found that, despite the legislated requirements and the structures and processes that both municipalities have in place to engage in community participation, these do not always work. Consultation is often seen as 'token' or 'time-consuming' and does not necessarily mean that residents have a meaningful contribution to government's planning and implementation.

The Town Planning Acts in most states of India provide for structures and processes to facilitate and enhance community involvement including community based integrated development planning. In addition, cities like Mumbai have elected ward councilors and ward committees,

Citizens are promised effective community participation through several legislative mechanisms including the 74th-75th amendment to the Indian Constitution, which focus on a range of socio-economic rights and promotes developmental, inclusive and participatory local government. The law requires local government to work with its citizens and communities. For example, ward committees are a forum for citizens to voice their concerns to promote community participation. Yet, community participation in housing-related decisions remains inadequate. In some cases poor people's housing strategies are in conflict with competing interests and authorities, and they are removed from settlements. Declaring their activities as "unauthorized" by the authorities increases their vulnerability, with non-local population particularly at risk.

Since 1995, when it was created, the Mumbai Slum Redevelopment Authority has consistently failed to put in place policies focused on in situ upgrading. In other words, improving informal settlements where people have already erected structures for shelter has been deliberately neglected.Slum re-housing continues to be built on poorly located land far from work opportunities and social facilities. In addition, the upgrading of informal settlements and provision of low-income rental units is almost non-existent. The recent cases in Mumbai, Delhi and some other cities where government demolished houses built by residents who were duped by fraudsters into buying illegally secured land, reveals the extent of the shortage of land for affordable housing in Indian cities.

There is a growing problem of homelessness and inadequate housing. This huge demand for housing has led to the poor resorting to "illegal" occupation of dilapidated buildings in inner cities like Mumbai causing frequent structural collapses and human fatalitiesIn Mumbai, most dilapidated old buildings are poorly maintained "chawls" usually in the inner city, which threaten the health and safety of occupants. Mumbai has approximately 16000 dilapidated (cessed) buildings of which only about 1200 have been reconstructed since 1999.

Location of housing remains critical as economic opportunities for the poor are so important. Poor people try to locate close to areas where they can find economic opportunities, which often bring them into conflict with the local authority. Various social surveys by NGOs in the slums of cities in India (and in the Author's own experience of interaction with project affected families in world Bank aided projects in Mumbai and Chennai) highlighted the availability of employment opportunities, transport networks and schools as key motivations for the location of housing for resettlement of slum residents.

At the same time, local government is faced with serious urban management challenges, particularly those linked to housing. Municipalities do not have adequate funding and capacity to deliver physical services. Court cases that have followed evictions of families from dilapidated structures and illegal slums have only further underlined the fact that there is an urgent need to provide options to these families living in intolerable conditions, by considering in situ upgrading and provision of alternative accommodation.Cities must make explicit commitments in their development plan making process to make public participation an integral part of the planning, budgeting and service delivery processes. City development process must work with the people to plan for their future rather than merely informing the community of what is going to happen to them. Community participation processes should be seen as a genuine attempt at capturing the developmental aspirations of the people and not merely a public affirmation or a checklist exercise.

Community participation for residents living in dilapidated buildings marked for redevelopment and in informal settlements is inefficient where it exists, and non-existent in most cases. In fact, in cities like Mumbai the only interaction the slum residents have with the authorities is when the police or officials of the local or Slum Redevelopment Authority harass them for identity documents. The drive for "Adhar" cards should in fact be concentrated and taken up vigorously in the dilapidated buildings and slum areas of cities like Mumbai. There is a perception that politicians only seek out such communities during the election period. What is their interaction in the so called participatory mechanisms for local development? In the affected people's eyes, the enforcement of municipal by-laws seems to be the only feature of municipal-community interaction!

The civil society organizations, rather than engaging themselves in national corruption issues, could instead, fight for the "right to participate" in the city development process. In the absence of any such initiative, mass protests, demonstrations and approaching the "news hungry" TV media have often become the outlets for people's expression of frustration. A key issue is the importance of effective communication. When considering housing options for the poor it is important that issues around participation of the poor are addressed in conjunction with those affected. Far more emphasis should be placed on effective communication with ward councilors, NGOs and residents.

The New Paradigm

The Statement of Industrial Policy, 1991 that heralded India's economic liberalization stated "Government will continue to pursue a sound policy framework.... spread of industrialization to backward areas of the country will be actively promoted through appropriate incentives, institutions and infrastructure investments."

This high sounding statement was a precursor to establishment of the Special Economic Zones. These SEZs, in time, became the authorized land grab by private entrepreneurs gobbling up the agricultural lands and uprooting and throwing the agriculturists out of the only skills that he knew for generations and filling up the cities with the migrants divested of their agricultural lands and income.

Why did the "great" Indian urban planners never tiring of advocating land assembly schemes not think of applying the same principle to the establishment of SEZ by making the farmers active partners in the projects that would have given

81

them a prosperity linked income along with a minimum homestead land to carry on agricultural occupations like vegetable farming and dairy development?

"India lives in villages" an oft-repeated adage needs to be modified to read 'India dies in its villages"

Are Indian Cities Crumbling?

After decades of being a nation of rural dwellers, Indians are rapidly moving into cities in search of better jobs, but the housing infrastructure is not keeping pace. The lack of action to relieve the housing crisis in India's cities seems certain to undermine the country's efforts to 'vault its multitudes out of poverty and share the fruits of its nearly double-digit growth more widely,'.

A recent McKinsey report stated that in order to accommodate the massive forecasted urban growth, India would have to build the equivalent of the city of Chicago every year. But no such plans have arisen. Instead, cities are buckling under the strain and illegal housing developments are literally falling apart under the strain of demand.

"The dilapidated state of Indian cities is in some ways by design. For decades, Indian governments tried to discourage migration to cities by making city life unaffordable and unbearable for new arrivals." Now that India's rural populations have voted with their feet, their cities need to catch up. The article appears based upon inadequate & misinformation mostly restricted to conditions in Delhi. It credits the government with intelligence and perspective that it does not have.

To claim that the " the dilapidated state of Indian cities is in some ways by design. ... Indian governments tried to discourage migration to cities by making city life unaffordable and unbearable for new arrivals." is to draw erroneous conclusions from the chaotic urban planning scenario in India. To claim that " these policies were driven at least in part by a Gandhian belief that India should be a rural nation, and more broadly by a centrally planned, socialist approach to development." is to display abysmal ignorance of and misunderstanding of the Gandhian philosophy..Statements like "the number of floors in most neighborhoods is capped at five stories, and in many areas fewer. The government largely controls land, and government approval for new development is difficult to obtain, even to house the wealthy and middle class, never mind the poor" obviously relate to conditions in Delhi and not other cities in the country.

To state that, "the current building codes wouldn't allow me to do it profitably.....there is a demand that is not being met, and the only way to meet it is by breaking the law." is to clearly display ignorance of current state of building bylaws in the cities in the country and again is based on the Delhi experience only. It is more than 30 years that building regulations in India were tailored to suit development of low income housing. I was my self instrumental in getting a new building code (IS 8888 1974) introduced by the then Indian Standards Institution to facilitate development of small affordable houses/apartments.

To state that, "as miserable as living conditions in city slums and tenements might be, they are much better than the ones villagers leave behind. ... a recent government report said 65 percent of villagers lacked toilets, while only 11 percent of city dwellers did. Cities also have much better access to piped water and proper sewage" is to display a complete ignorance of the rural ecology and again restrict oneself to conditions in Delhi. If a report says that only 11% of city dwellers lack toilet facilities it is obviously unaware that in Mumbai more than 65% of population lives in slums having meager toilet facilities.

What are slums? Slums are not the physical edifices. Slums are people. Who are these people?They are the ones pushed out from hinterland or even from faraway lands (as In case of Metropolis like Mumbai) who, cannot find livelihood in their own region or are attracted by the lure of city life, or want better compensation for work or have no land to till or their skills do not have adequate demand or are outcasts/fear for their life in a caste dominated environment

Why are they pushed out?

Inadequate economic opportunities, or Craving for "city life" or Surplus of labour & skills in their region or Fragmentation of land making agricultural holding uneconomic or have no skills other than farming orhounded out by opportunists, politicians, terrorists, upper caste echelons.

How to stop the migration to cities? Spend more on rural development in terms of farming technology, agro based industries, physical. socio-economic and health infrastructure to contain the migration to cities

Why the planners did not wake up to this problem early? Had there been intelligent and perceptive thinking, cities could have established reception centres on peripheral areas providing Migrant reception centres in cities:Why the city governments and "sites & Services" like facilities with adequate transport and may be avoided the squatting on public lands . Even today the only response to the problem is to "regularize" the squatter colonies

Regularization: incentive to further squatting?

Political compulsions of creating vote banks led to regularization of squatter colonies and the word spread among the migrant community that squatting on public lands is the best way to get a free home! So it gave a further impetus to migration

Bankruptcy of vision or deliberate neglect of the problem?

Whatever be the reason, the private initiative was quick to realize the "potential" of the squatters as agents to get cheap land. It was rumored that some unscrupulous builders maintained large number of migrants as paid squatters to squat on private lands where after they would offer the owner of the land to get the squatters evacuated if sold the land at a cheap price to the builder

The state/local government wittingly or un- wittingly played in the hands of the developers by announcing the SRA schemes which gave a bonanza by way of disproportionately increased FSI to the developers if they built free houses for the occupants, Just to illustrate , land cost being nil, the cost of a 225 sq. ft slum dwelling with infrastructure, even today does not exceed Rs. 2.5 laks to recover which the builder needs to build only 20 sq. ft (assuming the free flat is sold at rs. 12000 per sq. ft.). It means that the FSI could be increased only by 1/10 of the existing one. which is 1. Yet, invariably, in SRA schemes FSI in excess of 4.5 is granted

Building of the Towers

The result is the building of the luxury towers bringing in astronomical profits to the developer but loading the local government with the responsibility of providing services, transport, parking etc to the new development. AND this rich class requires domestic services providing a further incentive for increased migration to the city. The vicious circle continues.

What are the options?

Slum improvement –providing minimum essential services like water, drainage, public sanitary facilities and electricity is one option that will not add to the population or load on the services of the local government. Hyderabad has tried it by giving land tenure to the squatters. The greatest disadvantage of this option is that it does not bring glory to the politician or the Bureaucrats and development authorities neither does it transform Mumbai into Shanghai. But those who talk of such transformations and are over enthusiastically implementing SEZs (idea borrowed from China where there is no private ownership of land) seem to forget that China is a totalitarian state.

December 2010

"Political compulsions of creating vote banks led to regularization of squatter colonies and the word spread among the migrant community that squatting on public lands is the best way to get a free home!"

India Needs Futuristic Policies to manage economic growth and rapid urbanization

With the recent rapid strides of the Indian economy, acceleration in the urbanization trend can be safely predicted. Every economy undergoing such rapid growth has witnessed higher levels of urbanization akin to what is taking place in China. Do India's towns, cities and metropolitan centers have the institutional structures and resources to manage this transition?

Even if urbanization is an inevitable outcome of fast economic growth, should the policies be formulated at the expense of building sustainable rural communities? Or should the policy interventions be targeted to create a system with centers of prosperity spread across the country? What could be pillars of the country's urbanization policy?

Creating multiple centers of prosperity

It is easy to view urbanization as the root cause of malaise affecting India's cities. The country therefore needs to tailor urbanization policies to create a harmonious interface with our rural areas. Urban centers have the advantage of economies of scale and scope in offering a range of services to the citizenry that are uneconomical to provide in the vast rural hinterland. The percentage of India's urban population is close to only 30 per cent. Within this segment, the vast majority in concentrated in Class I cities and especially in large metropolitan cities. This has led to unbalanced development wherein metropolitan areas are becoming ungovernable with uncontrolled growth, and smaller cities lack the wherewithal to deliver even basic services.

This calls for a two-pronged approach where planners focus on consolidating growth and delivering better services to people in metropolitan areas but at the same time plan and develop new, smaller cities to become the engines of future growth. But given the socio-political structure that has emerged in established metropolitan cities, where competing power centers jostle for resources and influence, the task of bringing real change is difficult and could be painstakingly slow.

The options available to planners in this sphere range from building satellite townships, creating new planned cities and managing the growth of rapidly expanding cities through investments in institutional capacity building, developing industrial corridors and even building private townships where even the traditional municipal functions can be privately managed. We need to evaluate and follow appropriate for optimizing the full range of opportunities available to us.

Cities need to fulfill the economic, security, environmental, spatial, and other needs of people to create a sense of identity and build long-term sustainability. An essential step in this process is the creation of an enabling environment and a long-term global policy so that successive governments (irrespective of their political hue or ideology) take an ecosystem-centric view of urban development. For the cities to harness the human potential of the urban immigration, they must focus not only on promoting industries that take advantage of the opportunities available but also on taking steps to create new opportunities

India needs to expand the options available to people so that the large metros do not remain the only meaningful choice available to live an urban life. For the foreseeable future though, the large metros may continue to play a dominant role in the national economy and in creating a vast marketplace that will be at the apex of a multi-tiered, India urban system. The trends in recent years have shown a city like Delhi, which has a large degree of control over the generation and usage of funds, has had far better outcomes than places like Mumbai, which fill the coffers of the state government but do not get commensurate investments back. Cities are India's greatest assets and we have the opportunity to either harness the urbanization trend to create more centers of prosperity or go down the path of metro-centric growth, which can lead to an urban disaster.

Urban development and economic growth

There exists a dual relationship between economic growth and urbanization, while urbanization is an important side effect of economic growth, it is at the same time essential to sustain economic growth. The Indian growth story however does not quite conform to this dictum. Despite India's recent rapid economic growth, the pace of urbanization has been slower than the economic growth. This is primarily a result of rural exodus to metropolitan cities, which have appropriated a large chunk of urban development resources, inadequate government policies, improper governance models, bureaucratic inefficiency, and lack of systematic urban planning. The problem being multi-faceted, requires multi-pronged solutions based on a critical analysis.

Urbanization in India is mostly oriented towards major cities, leading to the evolution of 'two India's ' the rich urban India and the poor rural India. The evolution of metro-centric growth and how it has affected the rate of urbanization are very important questions that may help in understanding how rural and urban economies interact to influence urbanization.

The rural economy in last few years has been highly unstable due to a decrease in agricultural productivity and lack of opportunities in the organized sector; urban centers on the other hand have witnessed rapid growth. This has resulted in skewed growth and a massive rural-urban migration. While the rate of migration increased, the rate of urbanization is not keeping pace and as a result cities other than metropolitan centres are no longer able to offer employment to all unskilled labor migrating from rural areas.

It is therefore imperative for a developing country like India to improvise an inclusive economic policy and link it with urbanization policy to reduce rural urban migration, which adversely affects urbanization. To this effect the government has tried to make amends by programs like Jawaharlal Nehru National Urban Renewal Mission (JNNURM) and the National Rural Employment Guarantee Act (NREGA) to facilitate inclusive and equitable growth, but the gap still persists.

What is required is economic empowerment of rural areas by reducing their dependence on agriculture and increasing the availability of opportunities in other organized sectors in rural settings; skills development and infrastructure improvement. This will facilitate growth of self sustaining rural economies capable of offering employment to rural laborers thus reducing rural-urban migration and making urbanization a broad-based phenomenon not restricted to metropolitan cities.

Another important issue which could facilitates rapid and efficient urbanization is 'decentralization of governance', especially devolution. This increases the accountability, responsiveness and ownership of local authorities and helps them tailor development activities, to local needs, thus speeding up the process of urbanization. The 74th Constitutional Amendment was enacted to implement this initiative. However, due to discretionary allocation of functions and insufficient allocation of executive control to the local authorities the local bodies have become ineffective, contrary to what was envisioned. Merely assigning the responsibility does not automatically enable local bodies to design projects and implement them. They require planning and resources support.

The government transferred developmental responsibility to local authorities without empowering them economically or raising their resource generating capacity. Though not a big issue for larger cities (due to better & larger recourse and access to state funds), it adversely affected smaller cities by increasing their dependence on external funds, which in turn affected infrastructure development thus limiting their growth. More over, the government has also failed to strengthen the management skills and capabilities of these bodies to help them manage this change. The government therefore needs to work towards delegating increased and substantial control to the local bodies, enhancing their skills to make this model of governance successful.

The government also needs to continuously and increasingly invest in infrastructure projects (transportation, electricity, water resource management etc.). This will enable equitable and sustainable urbanization and subsequent economic growth. This, however, requires financial planning (resource allocation) especially at the level of small cities and rural areas that are incapable of generating adequate funds for infrastructure projects. This can be achieved either through government funding, external institutional financing, or through community involvement.

What India needs is a futuristic urban policy that facilitates financial resource management, skills enhancement, improved governance, and infrastructure development- and not mere urban development; to tackle issues affecting India's urbanization process.

January 2011

The Emerging Asian City:

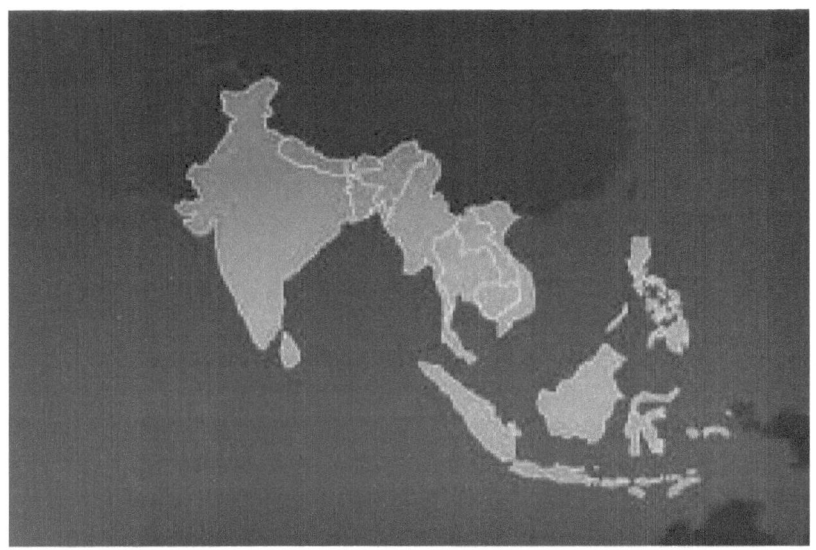

Do we need newer insights and provocations to broaden and deepen our understanding of urban Asia?

In fact there has been very little understanding of the truth about the genesis and evolutionary culture of urban Asia by the urban planners of the western world straight jacketed by their perceived concepts of urbanization and by the urbanists of the developing world blinded by visions of 'global village' and aping the western concepts of Urban growth..

Is there really any profound and sophisticated scholarship bringing Asia to the forefront of the mainstream dialogue? If there is, is it not percolating because it is restricted to the Academics unaware of the dynamics of the practicing fraternity?

Can any broadening of the discussion touch even the fringes of a rational approach to urban development mired as it is particularly in India, in the corrupt political environment & bureaucratic practices?

Not only the Asian urban but the universal urban landscape is shaped by distinct phenomena-social, political, economic and cultural; only the mix varies in its proportion of the 'ingredients' depending on the penetration of market economies in the urban culture of a country

Do Traditions, Tensions & Transformations deemphasize geographic themes in the current global market environment? These have now lost the context and meaning for differential tenor and hue of urban growth in the current market driven economies in the Indian scenario if not to a similar extent in Asian urban scene. In India the colonial cities reveal a struggle to retain native spatial concepts rather than amalgamate those in dwellings and monuments as a reaction to imposed "styles'.At least in Chandigarh the greatest lesson lies in demonstrating the utter failure and atrocity of imposing on the local climate, tradition and culture alien concepts and construction technique in the name of post modernism and its rejection demonstrated by what the city has become today

Navigating and transforming the existing processes for urban change towards equity and social justice demands total rejection of the pseudo "models" of Singapore or Shanghai and evolve approaches based on optimization of existing resources-fiscal human & management- to achieve cost effective urban development in India and the Asian countries.

7th Feb. 2013

"Is there really any profound and sophisticated scholarship bringing Asia to the forefront of the mainstream dialogue? If there is, is it not percolating because it is restricted to the Academics unaware of the dynamics of the practicing fraternity?"

94

How to vandalize a City Plan: Gandhinagar

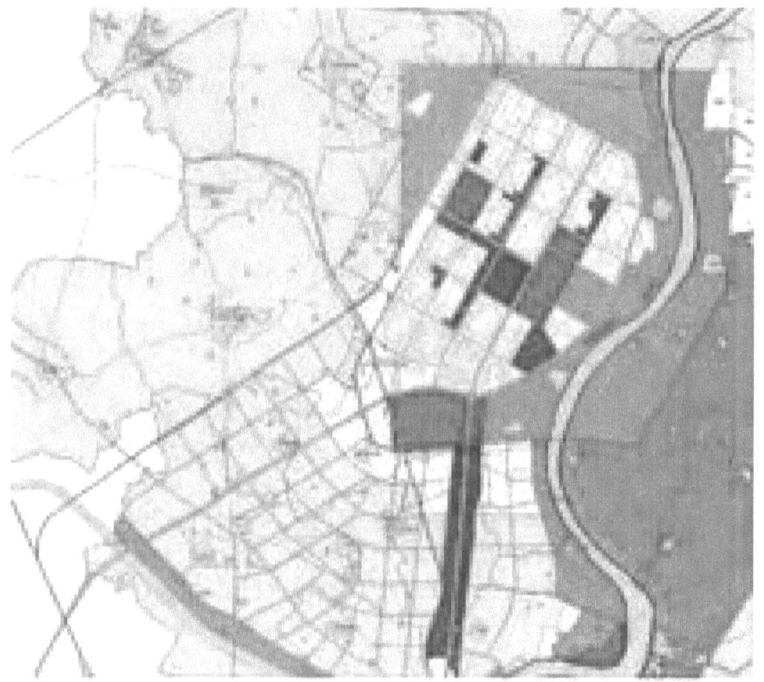

Consultants' proposed re-design of Gandhinagar, extending south like a comet's tail

The new capital of Gujarat-Gandhinagar-was planned by two Indian planners, H.K.Mewada and P.M.Apte and constructed between1965-1970. An influential group of architects from Ahmedabad with active support from some industrialists tried to usurp the job by bringing in American architect Louis Kahn, who was then in Ahmedabad to design the buildings of the management institute. The state government however stood firm and had the city designed by the two Indian town planners in the best traditions of Gujarat's rich heritage of town planning and principles of Mahatma Gandhi who had his "Ashram" south of the proposed site of the city on the banks of river Sabarmati.

The city was planned for a population of 150,000 but could accommodate double that number by increasing the floor space ratio from 1 to 2 in the areas reserved for private development. The river as the limit on the east, and the industrial area on the north, the most logical future physical expansion of the city was envisaged towards the north-west. Hence, as a rational extension of the city grid, the planners had envisaged 30 additional residential sectors (see plan below) to the northwest that could accommodate a population of 450,000. Thus, the growth potential of the city by densification and area expansion to the northwest is for a population of 750,000. To retain the identity of the city as a new town and the capital, the planners provided for its growth *away* from the city of Ahmedabad.

Unfortunately, the consultants appointed by the Gandhinagar Urban Development Authority (GUDA) have ignored this rationale and replanned the expansion of the city to the south. They perhaps saw that the lands between the two cities have a great market value that could be profitably exploited through private developers & hence managed to get the periphery control act abolished. The consultants did not review the original city plan nor did they consult the planners of the original master plan, thus eliminating the possibility of informed and constructive criticism. The consultants appeared to be driven by profit motive, raising serious doubts about their honesty and integrity. A southward expansion proposed by the consultants will merge the new city with Ahmedabad and finally make it its suburb, effacing its distinct identity.

What is the real objective of the redevelopment proposal prepared by the consultants of the Gandhinagar Urban Development Authority (GUDA)? Why do they want extension of the new Capital of Gandhinagar towards southwest (Ahmedabad) with radiating roads from the junction of 'GH' and 'J' roads? Is it to locate a 'New' Capitol /Sachivalaya Complex there? Such a proposal will obliterate the identity of

Gandhinagar's present Capitol complex which has won the "Best Architectural design" Award of the Indian Institute of Architects!

Architecture is considered the mother of all arts. It ought to be revered above personal prejudices. If an architect happens to dislike a building design, he should not go about destroying it like a terrorist! If architects went about dismantling the buildings or plans that they didn't like, it is sacrilege of the noble profession of Architecture! But such ethical considerations do not seem to deter the new breed of consultants! This conclusion is buttressed by the manner in which the consultants of GUDA have charted a redevelopment plan for Gandhinagar. The plan proposes to demolish Gandhinagar's identity as a capital. The consciously designed axial plan is sought to be dismantled. Now the buildings of the capitol complex are also not to be spared!

The proposals raise serious doubts about the morality, sincerity and professional ethics of the consultants. Had Gandhinagar been designed by Louis Kahn or Le Corbusier, would they have dared to make such proposals? If the city is to be expanded and extended, it could have been done as originally envisaged; towards north-west (as depicted below) in keeping with the original plan, retaining the urban design concept and the central vista (Road no.4).

Figure 4 Master Plan. Future Expansion

97

Original plan showing future expansion and extension.

In Gandhinagar's original plan its future expansion was envisaged to the northwest to maintain and continue the 'axis', focusing on the Legislative Assembly building. The consultants have deliberately proposed its extension to the south to completely destroy the most important and monumental concept of the central vista (Road No. 4) that focuses on the capitol complex and was to be extended naturally to the northwest, maintaining the axis and expanding the city physically in that direction. Consequently, the location of a Gandhi memorial on this axis, on "J" Road as originally provided, is now proposed to be near the railway station!! But the consultant's intentions appear not just dismantling the city's plan but also to:

1. Completely obliterate the axial planning by permanently stopping the future expansion to the northwest and instead proposing it to the southwest towards Ahmedabad.

2. Deface and destroy the capitol complex by:

    a. physically demolishing the connecting bridges between the Assembly building and the Secretariat blocks on either side of it;
    b. filling up the space so created with office buildings 'crowding' the Assembly building into insignificance and oblivion, and;
    c. scrapping the grand 'Mughal Garden' at the rear of the Assembly building and instead locating there an unsightly electric grid station.

3. Destroy the capitol complex group of buildings and thereby create an opportunity to design a new Secretariat Building perhaps at the apex of the radiating road pattern to the southwest proposed in their redevelopment plan for Gandhinagar.

Let us examine how the intended defilement of the Capitol Complex is to be achieved:

1   Demolish the bridges between the Assembly building and the Secretariat building on either side of it:

In the original plan (as already constructed) the State Assembly building is flanked by the Secretariat buildings on either side, connected to it by two bridges (see photograph below). The bridges facilitate easy physical communication for the ministers, Legislators and secretaries to the Assembly precinct without moving out of the building. This 'green' and low carbon footprint link is now proposed to be physically broken down and the space between the Secretariat building and the Assembly building filled with some office buildings – so crowding the site that the identity of the State Legislature building will be lost and it may not even be visible as a distinct edifice!

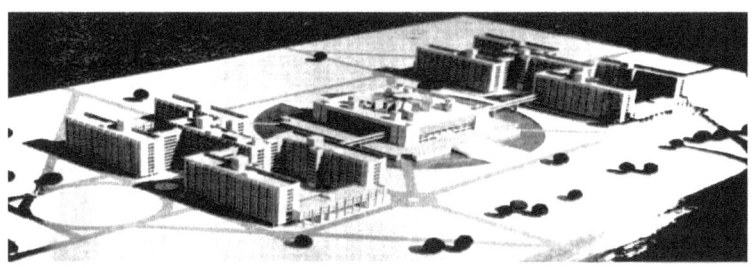

Capitol Complex (model) showing the bridges connecting Assembly building with secretariat on either sides.

Thus, the consultants can make an issue of the "lost identity" of the State Legislature building and press for a new building to be designed by them! If this excuse in itself was not convincing, one more defilement has been proposed:

2. Defacing the Legislature Building by destroying the large landscaped garden behind it (stretching up to the riverside 'J' Road) and instead building an electric grid station there!

99

In the original plan, the large area behind the Legislature Building was proposed to be developed into a beautiful ornamental garden like the 'Mughal Garden' adjoining the Rashtrapati Bhavan in New Delhi, lending grandeur and dignity to the building. This is now proposed to be scrapped.

3.Remove the Gandhi Memorial from its original location on the river bank and have it in front of the railway station at the end of the Road no.4 thereby permanently closing the central axis of the city plan and making the memorial into a mere 'statue' amidst the traffic of the railway station!

In the original plan, an imposing memorial to Mahatma Gandhi was proposed at a site behind the Capitol Complex, overlooking the Mughal gardens, on the banks of the river, across "J" Road on the axis of Road no.4. It would have formed an imposing backdrop to the Legislative Assembly building. Now it is proposed to be located in the petty commercial area near the railway station and will effectively block road no.4 destroying permanently the original axial plan and possibility of the originally intended future extension of the city toward north-west.

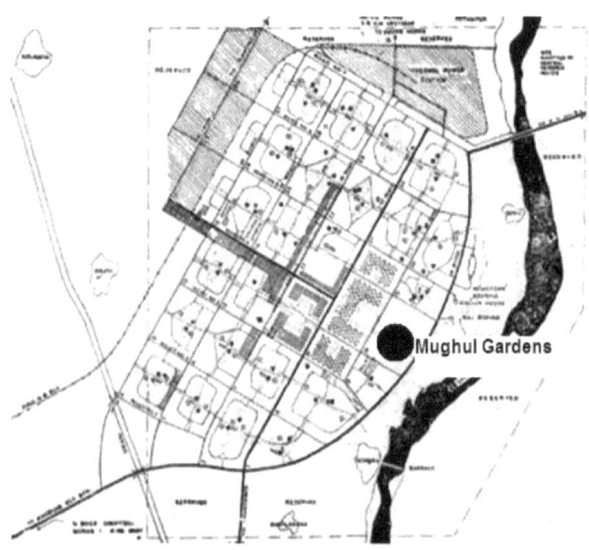
Mughul Gardens

At the end of the garden, across the 'J' Road, on the riverbank was proposed a monument to Mahatma Gandhi. Instead, consultants propose to build an electric grid station at the location of the Mughal Gardens, the towers and wires of which can be visible above the Legislative Assembly Building!

This would finally complete the total disfigurement of the entire Capitol Complex. It would then be possible for the consultants to convince the politicians and the bureaucrats of the complete unsuitability of the original Capitol Complex as the headquarters of a progressive state like Gujarat and the need to build a new Legislature and/or Secretariat building. Where else? Where they want, in between Gandhinagar and Ahmedabad!

The real purpose of the proposal of the consultants to extend the city towards southwest has now become clear. The idea is to radiate roads from the proposed location of the New Capitol Complex at the south of Gandhinagar near the junction of 'GH' Road and the 'J' Road so that the new Secretariat would be the first visual depiction of the new capital city as proposed to be reconstructed and built by the consultants. This seems like a 'sinister design' to destroy the identity of the original plan and the original Capitol Complex and in the process obliterate the identity of the city and its planners, Mewada and Apte, and glorify perpetually the name of the consultants.

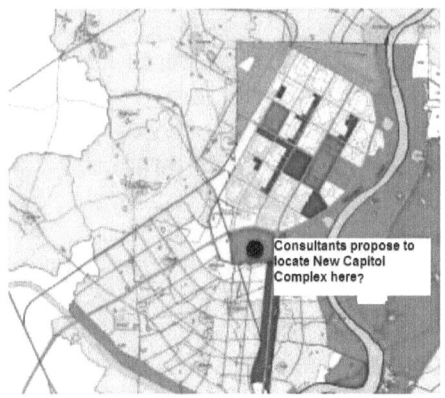

Does the proposed expansion of the city to southwest with radial roads have the hidden agenda for relocation of a new Capitol Complex to be designed by the consultants?

This 'Colossal Defacement' will also help to justify the geometry of the expansion plan of Gandhinagar as suggested by the consultants as the location of the 'New Capitol Complex' could then be at the confluence of the roads 'J' and 'GH' on which converge the radial roads proposed in the expansion of the city by the consultants. This would be like the last nail in the 'coffin' of Gandhinagar's original plan.

One suspects whether these proposals, that effectively destroy the original plans of the capital city have been cunningly put forward to pander to (a mistaken notion) the current state administration controlled by a political party that was not in power when the original plans for Gandhinagar were prepared and implemented between 1960 -1970? One has to concede the perverted ingenuity of this scheme! It reminds one, of the reconstruction plan prepared by Albert Speer for Berlin. This is Architectural and Town Planning terrorism of the worst kind that is being unleashed by GUDA consultants.

Placed in a somewhat similar situation, what action was taken by planners in Chandigarh? Le Corbusier designed the Secretariat, High Court, Legislative Assembly, and the Museum of Knowledge In Chandigarh. The international community of planners and historians is now campaigning in earnest to preserve this architectural legacy. The campaign is intended to press UNESCO to designate Chandigarh as a World Heritage Site and immediately take measures to prevent its defacement. The campaigners believe that strong statements of international concern may succeed where local outcry has not.

In this 42nd year of existence of the new capital of Gujarat,

Will the Architects & Planner's community in Gujarat and India similarly press UNESCO to designate Gandhinagar as a World Heritage site and urge the Gujarat Government to immediately stop and prevent its defacement by pseudo- consultants?

102

Will the government reintroduce the original "New Capital Periphery Control Act" (got scrapped by profit mongering dishonest consultants) to maintain the distinct identity of the new capital and stop the blatant exploitation, undesirable urbanization and unbridled development of the lands between Ahmedabad & Gandhinagar?

Will the Government invite an eminent and internationally acclaimed Indian architect like Charles Correa or Christopher Benninger to critically examine and evaluate Gandhinagar's redevelopment proposals by the GUDA consultants and advise the government on a sane & rational approach to redevelopment?

Will the progressive and enlightened government of this state put a stop to this wanton and malicious plunder of Gandhinagar's plan and defacement of its Capitol Complex by self seeking pseudo-consultants?

July 2012

Land Acquisition Compensation

When a large area of land is to be acquired for an enterprise-commercial or industrial- the compensation to be paid to the land owners assumes great importance.

To my mind, price and value are relative terms particularly in the context of Land which is a non- renewable source. One can look at it from the view point of the looser-the landowner- and the gainer-the one who stands to gain from the use of that land..So far, "Value" of land has been looked upon from the view point of the looser. Hence the concept of market price, opportunity cost, what one would have earned out of it etc. From the view point of the 'gainer' he may gain or profit many times more than the 'compensation' he may pay or even loose all! Hence as I have been propounding in case of SEZ, an optimum course would be to,

1. make a Town Planning. scheme and in a compact area with

existing access and nearness to infrastructure resettle free of cost all the land owners in plots large enough to build a house ,keep cattle, have a small vegetable garden and area for a workshop.

2   assemble   the   remaining   land   for   the   buyer.

3.   new titles be given to existing land owners for the plots allotted   to   them   without   any   payment   to   the   buyer

4 . Shares of the company formed by the buyer be given to the land   owners   in   proportion   to   their   land

5 . For the purpose of allotment of shares the value of land be taken as the prevalent market rate of land for NA purposes in the nearest urban agglomeration (any town declared as "Urban")

6..The land owners take the risk of prospering with the enterprise or   sinking   with   it

7 . The land owners can sellof their shares or trade those on the stock market and get cash

The Social Insecurity

An Architect has raised some pertinent questions about a nation's response to terrorists attack like the one on 26th November in Mumbai, India.

His comments that an aggressive response would obviously play into the hands of the masterminds of the terror..Such a response probably indicates his aversion to a 'tit for tat' reaction, though such a response may become necessary to ascertain and declare a nation's resolve to uphold its sovereignty and independence. If ".the attacks were clearly meant to be a provocation.." does he imply that Indians should not allow themselves to be "provoked" even after " a cosmopolitan area, home to19 million people and also the financial and entertainment capital of India was shaken.. "?

One would agree with him that "closing roads" etc. is a theatrical response that achieves little except causing inconvenience to the citizen and curbing use of recreational & other amenities. This is a Planner's point of view. But the same theatrical response (like road barriers, sandbags with machine gun totting commandoes etc) can help to instill a sense of security (even if false) and being "under protection" to the common citizens. Is it not as important?

No amount of security precautions and what the Architect calls "theatrical responses" can resolve the problem because a terrorist is a "dedicated' and fanatical individual who knows that he will not live through his suicidal mission. The only possible remedy is to have a very strong and intensive intelligence net work. to fore warn an impending strike

He said further ".war makes practical sense when you believe that you will cause more damage across the border.." We have to take into consideration the geo-political realities in the subcontinent. Despite its subdivision in to two nations of Pakistan & India in 1947, the former has never accepted the realities, not being able to overcome the hangover of the Mughal empire that ruled India before the British. With that hangover, Pakistan, since 1947, has waged 5 wars with India, of its own making and lost all of them most ignominiously! Despite its religious fanaticism it has the sense to appreciate that a nuclear war with India may destroy part of India but will physically annihilate Pakistan completely. So, what could be an option?

When examined in this perspective we should realize that what happened in Mumbai in November was not a random terrorist attack by a group (as is the case in many European countries like Germany, Spain, etc.) but a "Trial Run" of a state sponsored undeclared war ! If, just 10 well trained commandoes can hold a city of 19 million in terror why antagonize the whole world by waging a conventional war? Such a terror war instills a fear psychosis amongst the urban populace, shakes their confidence in its elected government. and creates doubts in the entire system of democracy and democratic governance!.

We need to realize and understand these geopolitical realities in the Indian sub-continent (which are unique and quite different from anywhere in the world except those that exist between Israel and its neighbors) before starting on a quest for planning solutions to terror threats in our Metropolitan areas.

106

It is a matter of deepest regret and misfortune for India that there is a large section of people who, despite any amount of solid proof and evidence that even a blind man could see, refuse to accept facts and continue to call Pakistan's undeclared war as exaggeration and making mountain of a mole hill! It is a measure of success for the Nehruvian misguidance of the Indian people reflected in the kind of statement made by the then Home Minister of Maharashtra that 'such SMALL incidences do keep happening in a large Metropolis!' The common people will ultimately pay with their lives for such blinkered thinking of the so called experts.

December 2000

Property Value Fixation

The present system of yearly fixation of stamp duty, area- wise, for properties in Mumbai was evolved to eradicate corruption that existed in determining the property value by favouring the parties to a sale deed by undervaluation and extract illegal gratification from them resulting in loss of revenue to the state government. The system leaves little scope for discretion or interpretation, thus minimizing possibilities of illegal gratification leading to rampant corruption that existed earlier.

The real modification required in the present system of 'Ready Reckoner" is to integrate a method of keeping parity with changing property values due to major factors like the current global melt down in economy. It would however appear that instead of a simple adjustment of the property value index, the meltdown is being used as an opportunity to reintroduce the earlier corrupt system of discretionary fixation of value to benefit all concerned including bureaucrats, politicians and builders!

"Urban planning as currently practiced in India is mostly for the benefit of the Politicians, Bureaucrats and the Developers. Development is merely a euphemism for land exploitation."

107

Corruption

Corruption is a universal phenomenon. It is not something new either. Corruption in one form or other existed since time immemorial. A review of penal codes in various ancient civilizations clearly demonstrate that bribery was a serious problem among the Jews, the Chinese, the Japanese, the Greeks and the Romans. As has been observed by some historians, corruption prevailed on a larger scale in India during the ancient period and the ones that followed.

One of the greatest evils of medieval administration in India was the extortion of perquisites and presents. Corruption was evident during the British rule in India. There was almost regular and systematic corruption involving almost all officials at different levels in the political and administrative hierarchy. There was an underlying belief among officials of "making hay while the sun of British Raj shone". If corruption has been an age-old phenomenon, a deep-rooted evil and a universal malady afflicting each and every society in one form or another at one time or other, then why is there so much concern now? Because, the present day corruption distorts competition, so denying the public access to the competitive marketplace. It induces wrong decisions resulting in: wrong projects, wrong prices, wrong contractors, substandard delivery, promotes corruption at lower levels and erodes public confidence in leaders. At lower levels, petty corruption is damaging because it adds to transaction costs, excludes those who cannot pay, fosters contempt for public servants and erodes capacity for revenue collection

Corruption in India has become a major issue. In its 2008 study, 'Transparency International' reports that 40% of Indians had firsthand experience of paying bribes or using a contact to get a job done in public office. In 2012 India has ranked 94th out of 176 countries in Transparency International's report, tied with, Colombia, Djibouti, Greece, Moldova, Mongolia, and Senegal.

The 'big scale' corruption scandals started in India as early as 1957 (Haridas Mundhra). This was followed by (to name a few) Nagarwala (1971), Antulay and cement (1982), Bofors (1989), Harshad Mehta (1992), palmolein oil imports in Kerala (1992), Telgi (1995), Sukhram and telecom (1996), fodder in Bihar (1996), Jain hawala (1997), Ketan Parekh (2001), ,Kargil coffins (2002), the Taj corridor (2003), the PDS scam in Arunachal (2004), oil for food (2005), Scorpene submarine deal (2006), stamp papers (2006), cash for votes (2008), Satyam (2008), Madhu Koda and mining (2009), 2-G (2010), Commonwealth Games (2010), Adarsh Housing Society (2010), housing loans by banking and financial institutions (2010), Belekiri port in Karnataka (2010), food grains in Uttar Pradesh (2010) and Bellary mines (2011). Westland Helicopters deal (2012). Corruption has become an issue in India because the big scale corruption has increased.

Role of Politics & Bureaucracy:

Some of the largest sources of corruption in India are entitlement programmes and social spending schemes of the government and include India's transport industry which is forced to pay billions in bribes annually to numerous regulatory and police stops on its interstate highways. Indian media has widely published allegations of corrupt Indian citizens stashing trillions of dollars in Swiss banks who, however, deny these allegations.

The causes of corruption in India include excessive regulations, complicated taxes and licensing systems, numerous government departments, each with opaque bureaucracy and discretionary powers, monopoly by government controlled institutions on certain goods and services delivery, and the lack of transparent laws and processes.

As of December 2008, 120 of India's 523 parliament members were accused of crimes, under India's First Information Report procedure wherein anyone can allege another of committing a crime. Many of the biggest scandals since 2010 have involved very high level officials of government, including Cabinet Ministers and Chief Ministers, such as in the 2G scam, the commonwealth games scam and the Adarsh Housing Society scam, Coalgate scam, mining scandal in Karnataka and cash for vote scam.

A 2009 survey of the leading economies of Asia, revealed the bureaucracy in India to be least efficient out of Singapore, Hong Kong, Thailand, South Korea, Japan, Malaysia, Taiwan, Vietnam, China, Philippines and Indonesia. It was also found that working with India's civil servants was a "slow and painful" process. In cities and villages throughout India, government officials, elected politicians, judicial officers, real estate developers and law enforcement officials, acquire, develop and sell land in illegal ways.

State-funded construction activities, such as road building, were dominated by construction mafias, which are groupings of corrupt public works officials, materials suppliers, politicians and construction contractors. According to The World Bank, only 40% of grain handed out for the poor reaches its intended target. The World Bank study finds that the public distribution programmes and social spending contracts have proven to be a waste due to corruption. The National Rural Health Mission programme has been clouded by large-scale corruption, waste and fraud-related losses which has been alleged to be Rs.100 billion!

Professor Bibek Debroy and Laveesh Bhandari claim in their book *Corruption in India:* that the public officials in India may be cornering as much as Rs.921.22 billion ($18.42 billion), or 1.26 per cent of the GDP, through corruption. The book claims, most bribery is in the transport industry, real estate and government delivered services. A November 2010 report from the U.S.A.-based 'Global Financial Integrity' estimates that over a 60-year period, India lost US$ 213 billion in illicit financial flows beginning in 1948; adjusted for inflation, this is estimated to be 462 billion in 2010 dollars, or about $8 billion per year ($7 per capita per year). The report also estimated the size of India's underground economy at approximately US$ 640 billion at the end of 2008 or roughly 50% of the nation's GDP. According to a third report, published in May 2012, Swiss National Bank estimates that the total amount of deposits in all Swiss banks, at the end of 2010, by citizens of India were CHF 1.95 billion (INR 92.95 billion, US$ 2.1 billion). The Swiss Ministry of External Affairs has confirmed these figures upon request for information by the Indian Ministry of External Affairs.

In a 2011 report on Corruption in India, one of the world's largest audit and compliance firms KPMG notes several causes that encourage corruption in India. The report suggests high taxes and excessive regulation & bureaucracy as a major cause. India has high marginal tax rates and numerous regulatory bodies with the power to stop any citizen or business from going about their daily affairs. This power to search and question creates opportunities for corrupt public officials to extract bribes; each individual or business decides if the effort required in due process and the cost of delay is worth not paying the bribe demanded. In cases of high taxes, paying off the corrupt official is cheaper than the tax. This, claims the report, is one major cause of corruption in India and 150 other countries across the world.

In real estate industry, the high capital gains tax in India encourages large-scale corruption. The correlation between high real estate taxes and corruption, claims the KPMG report, is high in India as well as other countries including the developed economies; this correlation has been true in modern times as well as for centuries of human history in numerous cultures. The desire to pay lower taxes than those demanded by the state explains the demand side of corruption. The net result is that the corrupt officials collect bribes, state fails to collect taxes for its own budget, and corruption grows. The report suggests regulatory reforms, process simplification and lower taxes as means to increase tax receipts and reduce causes of corruption.

Corruption is a disease. It may start as a reward, convert itself into a gratification, become a practice and with increase in cost of living, grow in size and content to keep up with ever growing need that converts itself into demand. Even after full satisfaction of the need it grows on its own 'fuel', ultimately converting itself into a disease. The greed to have more and more while motivating self improvement and progress in the initial stages later on converts itself into an addiction. The need for minimum food, clothing and shelter converts itself into a buffet spread of food, a vast wardrobe and palaces at different locations and countries. The gulf between the rich and the poor keeps widening and the resulting economic disparity in a country like India breeds violence, riots, discontent and social disharmony, giving further rise to moral, spiritual and religious corruption in the form of societal crimes, opportunistic god men and proliferation of edifices for so called religious beliefs.

'Happiness and contentment only comes from within and not from worldly riches' has been the teaching of the age old saints of every religion that is forgotten by enshrining them in gold and silver! A complete remaking of the moral fiber of our society is the only remedy for this deadly disease of corruption

Some of the largest sources of corruption in India are entitlement programmes and social spending schemes of the government

Terrorism

World Trade Center New York

The diabolic destruction of the Twin Towers in New York was an act as despicable as brazen. It was meant to be as much an affront as abuse. It sought to humiliate a great people and a great democracy into permanent shame.

Retaining the footprints of the towers as a 'memorial' and building a new Tower as a replacement would be more of a tacit and 'permanent' admission of the victory of the 'evil' over the 'good' than displaying a spirit of rejuvenation.

Architectural merits apart, the only definitive and forceful statement that a nation can make is to rebuild the Twin Towers exactly as they were and ensure that the cityscape and skyline of the great city is regenerated as if there was no aberration. A great people and a great democracy must demonstrate its undying character in 'immortality' of the symbols of its national ethos and not appear to be morally weaker than the forces of terrorism by grasping the opportunity for a new commercial exploitation of land and an Architectural commission.

November 2008 Terrorist attack on Mumbai: What should be a nation's response to terrorists attack like the one on 26th November in Mumbai, India?

Many claim that an aggressive response would play into the hands of the masterminds of the terror probably indicating an aversion to a 'tit for tat' reaction , though such a response may become necessary to ascertain and declare a nation's resolve to uphold its sovereignty and independence. If the attacks were clearly meant to be a provocation, should Indians not allow themselves to be "provoked" even after a cosmopolitan area, home to19 million people and also the financial and entertainment capital of India was shaken?

One may think that 'barricades and bunkers' are a theatrical response that achieves little except causing inconvenience to the citizen.. But this theatrical response (like road barriers, sandbags with machine gun totting commandoes etc) can help to instill a sense of security (even if false) and being "under protection" to the common citizens. Is it not as important?

No amount of security precautions and what may be called "theatrical responses" can resolve the problem because a terrorist is a "dedicated' and fanatical individual who knows that he will not live through his suicidal mission. The only possible remedy is to have a very strong and intensive intelligence net work. to fore warn an impending strike

We have to take into consideration the geo-political realities in the subcontinent. Despite its subdivision in to two nations of Pakistan & India in 1947, the former has never accepted the realities, not being able to overcome the hangover of the Moghal empire that ruled India before the British. With that hangover, Pakistan, since 1947, has waged 5 wars with India, of its own making and lost all of them most ignominiously! Despite its religious fanaticism it has the sense to appreciate that a nuclear war with India may destroy part of India but will physically annihilate Pakistan completely. So, what could be an option?

114

When studied in this perspective we should realize that what happened in Mumbai in November '08 was not a random terrorist attack by a terrorist group (as is the case in many European countries like Germany, Spain, etc.) but a "Trial Run" of a state sponsored undeclared war ! If, just 10 well trained commandoes can hold a city of 19 million in terror all it needs is a few hundred to devastate the whole of urban India! If a few well trained commandoes in the garb of 'Terrorists' can achieve its objective, why should Pakistan wage a formal war and antagonize the whole world?

Such a terror war instills a fear psychosis amongst the urban populace, shakes their confidence in its elected government and creates doubts about the entire system of democracy and democratic governance! That is the objective of such attacks by a terror state like Pakistan. Having successfully tested its new "Terrorists Weapon" that did not elicit any reaction except verbose appeals for peace, India can expect similar attacks on all its cities from Pakistan trained Commandoes in the garb of terrorists.

We need to realize and understand these geopolitical realities in the Indian subcontinent which are unique and quite different from any where in the world except those that exist between Israel and its neighbors.

Israel's   Biggest   Danger
The Editor, Newsweek

'Israel's Biggest Danger' By Fareed Zakaria (Feb. 23) shows striking similarities between the perception s of danger from the Arab minorities to Israel and the Muslim minorities to India. Muslim Indians have grown to over 151 m. (13.4%) from 38.85 m.(10.36%) in 1951 after India & Pakistan became two Nations and are estimated to be over 20% of country's population by 2020. Muslims enjoy all legal rights but not the obligations due to their "special minority status" and 'Islamic" beliefs. They do not accept the common civil code applicable to other Indians. Citizenship requires them only to be loyal to the law but not to the values or ideologies (secularism) of the state.

115

Hindu nationalists warn that India's Muslims constitute a demographic time bomb. For India, resolving issues of Muslim minorities is more crucial than dealing with Muslim terrorist groups and Pakistan. It will decide the future of India as a Secular State and a democracy.

March 2009

Your (Times of India)Editorial 'Heal Thyself' is bold and forthright. The Prime Minister "loosing his sleep at the trauma of the relations of a person detained for terrorist acts" could perhaps be understandable as his personal feeling in the context of unbridled Sikh bashing that his own party men and leaders indulged into after the assassination of Indira Gandhi, but its public expression by the Prime Minister of a country is almost anti national. It is definitely disturbing for its blatant and unabashed pandering to the Muslim community for political reasons. Such abetment of terrorism just because it is perpetrated by a minority religious community on whose electoral votes his party has an eye on, is nothing short of treason.

Your question is really the crux of the issue. Why are so many terrorists Muslims? Has Islam as a religion strayed from its original teachings of love, brotherhood and compassion to become an intolerant doctrine? The thinkers of Islam must have a serious introspection to urgently bring its followers back to the real teachings of the prophet.

State Home Minister on Mumbai Terror Attacks

It appears that our respected Home minister R R Patil normally enquires about the well being of his dear Kasab but had failed to do so in the last few days and though 13th july was Kasb's birthday the government did not send him a cake so his friends decided to give him a gift of 121 "cakes" and will give him an equal number of cakes in the next few days. The government better remember the birthday of Afzal Guru in jail sentenced to death by hanging awaiting for the last 5 years as the government is not happy about such harsh treatment to a pious man whose mercy petition to our great revered "Presidentess" is awaiting positive decision. Present fatal casualty is 121 which will certainly be revised to at least 249 as it is Kasab's 24th birthday

116

Even god cannot save a country whose so called leaders are hell bent on destroying it! (Kasab was finally hanged)

Hindu Terrorism

The real and the most important difference between the teaching of the so called Hinduism and most other religions is that Hinduism does not preach hatred neither does it exhort in the world that has resulted in drastic shrinkage of its sphere of influence (that extended to Indonesia, Malaysia, Thailand, Myanmar and other countries) and now restricted only to India. One is not a Hindu if he stoops to the level of the so called Jehadi terrorists and Talibans who consider the religion above the law of the country. There is no tenet in Hinduism against bigamy or multiple marriages-most ancient and modern Indian Hindu kings had any number of wives (Lord Krishna its followers to 'convert (to Hinduism) or kill'. It is in fact the most tolerant of the 'religions' is said to have had16000 wives!) Yet keeping in line with progressive thoughts and social imperatives, a Hindu majority national government enacted a law against Hindus having more than one wife and the Hindus accepted it without a murmur.

It should be noted that it is the so called Hindus and the Hindu political leaders who are clamoring for a ban on organizations like R.S.S. though similar non- Hindu organizations are allowed to preach hatred against Hindus because of the Hindu doctrine of tolerance and universal brotherhood. Since, Aseemanand has confessed to having aided and abated terrorism that killed a few (unlike the so called terrorist Kasab who has constantly protested his innocence- the innumerable witnesses and video and photographic evidence of his killing spree cannot be admitted as it is given by Hindus) he need not be tried in a court of law but can be immediately sentenced to death and hanged at the earliest. It is necessary before the Hindu majority political leaders and governments in order to pardon the already condemned Jehadi terrorists, enact a law to do away with capital punishment –with retrospective effect- as a proof of the Hindu tolerance towards those who kill wantonly in the name of religion. Jesus had in his last moments prayed to god to 'forgive them because they do not know what they are doing'. "They" should perhaps include the Jehadi terrorists. (Kasab was ultimately hanged).

The USA has shown that with determination and grit a nation can fight terrorism. How?

Seek out the terrorists where ever they are and destroy them. In this respect a nation has to be brute and ruthless. Irrespective of any consideration a nation must find those who wantonly kill innocent civilians in the name of religion and mercilessly annihilate them be they on foreign lands and territories. This lesson needs to be learnt particularly by pseudo-pacific nation like India.

"Let us remember that "Terrorism" is an anti-human barbaric act. It is neither Muslim nor Hindu!"

Epilogue:

There are many other issues, apart from PRUCT(Politics, Religion,Urbanization,Corruption,Terrorism) that ail this country. The most prominent being moral corruption. By corruption I do not mean it in the sense of graft but a serious erosion of the moral fibre of the society. It has naturally pervaded all classes of society, professions, trades, services etc. No aspect of living in this country is untouched by corruption. In fact it has become a way of life.

How does this corruption of the moral fiber of the society creep in? For a growing child its role models are firstly its parents, secondly its teachers and thirdly the visual & print media. A child's culture is subconsciously imbibed by its upbringing and not by 'culture workshops'. No amount of sermonizing can help a child if it is developing and formulating its beliefs, concepts and ideals in an environment wherein its parents are constantly seen compromising with circumstances by giving in to ethically wrong practices, teachers seem intent on training their wards to 'pass' examinations rather than gain knowledge and the media is glorifying lawlessness, graft and vulgar sex.

In 1948 immediately after India gained independence, My father was transferred to a new city where I had to be admitted to a new school. In the application form for admission, in the column meant to specify the applicant's religion my father wrote "Indian". It was not acceptable to the school administration which wanted him to write 'Hindu' and also mention the cast as "Brahmin". My father refused and I could not be admitted to the school. At the urging of his friends who feared for my education he had to finally relent. But he was a dejected man all his life. He did not perform my 'upanayan' ceremony so important for a Brahmin that it is considered as a second birth (hence the word "Dwij" – born twice applied to Brahmins). When later I asked him the reason his reply was "you will not become a Brahmin by wearing the sacred thread but by seeking knowledge and grasping it". This entire episode has left a lasting impression on my mind. I did not perform the thread ceremony for my two sons. In fact many years later a fine day I got a call from my elder son studying in USA asking me to which caste we belonged as most Indians asked him this question ! I feel, as a parent, I imbibed the right concepts in my sons.

My wife is an accomplished Hindustani classical singer. She thought she could teach and impart knowledge) which is considered as the holiest of 'gift'. At my insistence she agreed to charge Rs. 100 (this was in 1990) for 1wo hours of tuition. I have tried to tell her that even our maid servant's charges for menial job in our apartment is 200 Rs. per hour. But she views teaching as "imbibing culture" and not something to be imparted for a fee! The love and respect she gets from her students convinced me that next to the parents a Teacher is the best person to impart and imbibe good cultural and social values in the minds of the students.

And what has our print & Visual media done to further the spread of humane socio-cultural values? The actors on the screen and television are worse than the common prostitute who 'satisfy' a very limited number of 'customers! The 'item number' performers, almost naked on the screen, titillate and pander to the sex hunger of millions of viewers while a 'puritan' home minister of Maharashtra goes hammer and tongs after the 'Bar' girls who perform the same dances but fully clad in sarees! An entire generation of this country is being corrupted and vitiated beyond repair by our current breed of small and big screen cinema and the 'serials'. We now have even toddlers performing the item numbers in the little champ shows while their mothers look at them with great adulation and admiration!

In the ultimate analysis, who is to blame? Not the parents, not the teachers neither the media; we the people of this country are responsible for the abysmal down fall of all moral values in our socio-cultural environment! Why do we vote for the so called corrupt leaders? Why do we offer bribes to the policeman, the municipal official and others? Why do we flock to the assembly of pseudo religious men and 'Babas'? Why do we not observe simple road discipline or respect for our senior citizen? Why do we throw garbage on the road? It is we the people who are to be blamed squarely.

What ails India is Politics, Religion, Urbanization, Corruption and Terrorism but above all, the self seeking attitude of its so called educated urbanites. We have education but no culture. And to emulate culture we have no role models anymore! The real role models like Lokamanya Tilak, Subhashchandra Bose, Mahatma Gandhi, veer Savarkar, Lalbahadur Shastri have been imprisoned in marble statues and we now have 'charagate' and 'coalgate' fame politicians, corrupt cricketers and so called actors as the role models for the youth of this country! Yet, there are in the remote nooks and corners of this country Anna Hazres, Baba Amtes, and some selfless youth working for the poor and down trodden of this country without aspiring for name, fame or wealth! Because of them, India that is Bharat is still alive and may yet achieve resurgence like the Phoenix!

About the Author

Prakash M. Apte, born in 1939, is a graduate in Architecture, has a Masters in Regional Planning, a Diploma in Urban Design from Naples University, Italy. and a Diploma in Business Management.. He is a Fellow of the Indian Institute of Architects, & the Institute of Town Planners, India.

He led a team in 1965, to design and build the new capital city - Gandhinagar - for Gujarat state. Later as Chief of HUDCO (Housing & Urban Development Corporation of India) he executed over 250 housing projects. In 2004 he was invited by the Royal Government of Bhutan as a Senior Adviser for the Shelter Sector project for the Capital city Thimphu. He participated in the drafting of the Housing Sector paper for the 8th five year plan of India, and has been a Consultant for World Bank funded Low Income Housing programmes in Malaysia Gujarat, Madhya Pradesh, Maharashtra.& Tamilnadu.

From 1999 he was a consultant to the World Bank aided resettlement and rehabilitation project for Mumbai Urban Transport Project (MUTP) & Tsunami Emergency Rehabilitation Project at Chennai. He was invited as the 1988 Eisenhower Fellow from India by the Eisenhower Exchange Fellowships Inc. U.S.A. in the field of Urban Management.

He is the author of the books "The building of Gandhinagar, New Capital of Gujarat", "Urban Planning & Development, An Indian Perspective" and "Urban Growth Strategies; Mumbai Lessons".. A progressive thinker, he has written extensively in English & Marathi Newspapers about socio-political-cultural issues facing the country and his writings can be seen on his website www.angelfire.co/indie/pmapte/. The essence of his thinking on the socio-political-economic issues facing the country is reflected in this book, "What Ails India".